The Masses

Also by Giles Goodland

Objects on Hills
Littoral
Overlay
A Spy in the House of Years
Capital
What the Things Sang
The Dumb Messengers
Gloss

Giles Goodland

The Masses

Shearsman Books

First published in the United Kingdom in 2018 by
Shearsman Books
50 Westons Hill Drive
Emersons Green
BRISTOL
BS16 7DF

Shearsman Books Ltd Registered Office
30–31 St. James Place, Mangotsfield, Bristol BS16 9JB
(this address not for correspondence)

www.shearsman.com

ISBN 978-1-84861-561-8

Copyright © Giles Goodland, 2018.

The right of Giles Goodland to be identified as the author
of this work has been asserted by him in accordance with the
Copyrights, Designs and Patents Act of 1988.
All rights reserved.

Acknowledgements
Some of these poems have previously been published in
and/or, Blackbox Manifold, BlazeVox, Capilano Review, Ctrl + Alt + Del, Dalhousie Review, Glasfryn Project, interlitQ, Litmus, Long Poem Magazine, Magma, Molly Bloom, Node, para·text, Poetry Review, Poetry Wales, The Rascal, Tears in the Fence, The Wolf, Upstairs at Duroc, and in the *Aquanauts* anthology (Sidekick Books), often in very different forms.
Thanks to all of the editors concerned.

Thanks also to Geoff Sawers for offering valuable insights into an earlier version of this poem, and to Steven Hitchens for publishing some of the prose passages as 'from The Masses' as LPB Micro no. 9.

Contents

I. Vertebrates

The Slow Worms	11

II. Invertebrates

Silverfish	12
Mantis	14
Stick Insect	16
Harvestman	17
Chrysalis	18
The Moths	19
Cinnabar Moth	21
Clothesmoth	22
Hawkmoth	24
Ant	25
Soldier Ant	28
Wood Ant	29
Wasps	30
Hornet	33
Ichneumon	34
Caterpillar	35
Inchworm	36
Butterfly	37
Cabbage White	38
The Earwigs	40
Bees	42
Bumblebee	46
Honeybee	47
Flea	48
Caddis	50
Leatherjacket	51
Bot	52
Maggot	54
Grub	55
Nymph	56

Oak Gall	58
Bluebottle	59
Daddy Longlegs	60
Dragonfly	62
Dung Fly	63
Horsefly	64
Greenfly	65
House Flies	66
Unnamed Fly	68
Hoverfly	69
Lacewing	70
Midges	71
Mosquito	73
Stonefly	75
Scorpion	76
Pseudoscorpion	77
Tic	78
Silkworm	79
Woodworm	80
Thrips	81
Cockroach	82
Dung Beetle	83
Glowworm	84
Ladybird	85
Whirligig Beetle	88
Museum Beetle	89
May Bug	90
Sexton Beetle	91
Stag Beetle	92
Japanese Beetle	94
The Spider	95
Blood Spider	99
Garden Spider	100
House Spider	101
Funnelweb	103
Aphid	104
Hairlouse	105
Woodlouse	106
Pondskater	108

Cricket	109
Grasshopper	111
The Locusts	113
Slug	114
Bookworm	115
Bedbug	116
Snail	117
Millipede	118
Giant Millipede	119
Sandhopper	120
Crab	121
Worm	123
Threadworm	124
Sea slug	125
Leech	126
Tapeworm	127

III. Stone

Paper Shale	129

*In memory of Helen Kidd,
friend, teacher, enemy of the semi-colon.*

The Slow Worms

She kept an old piece of carpet over
the compost and when you lifted it
the pipework recoiled into intestinal
heat. Longated potentates graved ceramic
silvers upon the molded potato, among
ash heavings they forthcame to ingest hummus-
crumbs. When musics branched in this might of eye,
unlooking faces were named: asker
blet slayworm slew slorry or slow cripple.
Retained as a ghost word: properly slawerm,
or from schleichen, to creep, from soi-distant
slaha the smiter. Singleleggedly down herepaths
they wended the stews past madameve's.
This was not blindness to be in coil with,
coiting in a wood of desire, the intercourse
in their case of long duration, breath held head
for sense where surged the risk-averse
photophobe, beakerfolk of darkfold, spoking
through their sleep-crowned masks
upearthing the groundwound, viewing the light
of a stone that comes apart, glottus of molehill-
hole, nostrilled flute of the sorepoint they smelt
of sleep through eating out the edges of time,
where sifted the raingodsent clouds
even without the night-crying shrews that
grubbed where onions bulbed and moles degraded
underlawn, where coldcocked worms sophistically
browsed under henbane and sludged in-death
splendours, within leg of loveamour as
duskrain evedammed the blackbird-crowned sky
at ringing of raindusk they strayed
themselves askew in forms grosser than
huge, plumping with stained tactility.
Then she moved house again, and they remained.

Silverfish

I.

You are the ghost of a soul:
ghoul, undertile sliver,
quickthinking bringer of
decay: you have scale and
flourish in cadastral lines.

Fishscale, skinflake, atom
of neglect, dust aliving
and burst silence fits
this keyhole, idea of flight has
ego of a bird inside.
Scaled and feathered up,
you might fly from other moons.

A seep through which events unhappen
is widening. You arrive from
an unparallel world, disjoint in
code operating against
protocol, language of legs,
the meant-to-be unseen moment
fleshing under the skirting.

Zipped into fridgelit chitin
you prepare tomorrow's decay,
already building on the not-yet
torn down. In its place,
a person leans to the side.
All skin, he wants everything.

II.

The wallpaperpasteating cattle of the future
will break letters to see what they contain.
Imirage this tined extermite, in its
secreative niche-inch of finishy
shimmaterial alloyed of liquick.
It flowrests its fungible tuning
fork in twilist of metal-illness
like a scalextrix sleepulchre
ungumming in derivulets, thusly
it eareyes its fantennae, distrusks,
wraparounds the suturistic wordproofing
connecting sinuses & sunrises, synapses
& pinnacles. Home is where the Hoover
moans, and the sugar-guest camps in the map.
When they built the first house
it was already there, underearth salt
flake, subaltern of gristle flecking our floors.
Spleak machinese? In the city are signs
of habitation. To grow nameless
locate spacefolk in full slivery for whom
light is a faint material that points us in
to a room and pulls substantial ghosts
inwards. These are family, they can be
touched and will not retract when they come to
grains of sense. The dust exceeds the progeny
we understood the dream to mean.

Mantis

I.

He laughed his head off then he laughed
her head off. His fishhook arms
ran inhere behind the headline
to a zoo of coughs, a soukh of sky.
Beware the intellect of hunterland
the blublooded arm of state that razor
bleeds thumbends when the upstart shadow
break snickers on a lostlit subway stone
like the separate poor, harmless to leaves
but strippedown for a fight. Grand but
unsubstantiated claims were
made, empires lost at toss of coin,
ownlabel productlines postponed.
He was disinterpreter of dreams
in the light that takes place behind the eyes.
He felt broken into syllables
a novel aspiring hornlike across his skin
fleshwilled its uncountable midnights
into words to ask what was it that
had been sleeping inside me?
He woundup the flowerboned blackjacks
and angeltrod the log of the totenbuch.
Death gathered under the eyes of
the soothsayer in the deathheaded staffcar
strutting the very-legged tonguestone
to build the new world in your eyes he
tendered his forerearms and titular head
statued in giacometrized highstep the
christaline hormoniums clickclacked in
his notwithstandingless rostrum:
wounded by music the failed objects
rise from thoughts' torsion.
Time is our metaphor, flightpath, refuture.

II.

Stop in the law of the name, opal-eyed
zoomorph I saw you handle that
metaforknife, selfmake a mantic
remandible, jackknife a clerical
gesture, bury an incisive scalpel
in an unindexed future stakeholder,
stick to the script as treed females
command above reglistening cars.
You shot the serif but vulnerable
to thought's weaponry faced retaliation
ships scabbards kerned the cochleal evertheless
the civil world stuck the black bone down
the throat fired a transtantric cellcall
encysted the twiglit stingerend
to widerstand godswill in timescore
as a lifeskills orchestrator who
folksung the eyeshot sleepartist's revery-
thing, wind out praise sequent to intention
to write up reflection, engage pulse's
witness with Dante's intuitive head.
Here are the details of the song. A too
regular form beats on itself a grave
for the sake of symbol the quotes set
repulsion into coalescence
untouching a thrustable supper
clothed in the surfaeces of words, their
upprearances could be inceptive.
You are slender but must be vicious
to hold up the sky, the mind swings by
a grass-blade; irons while the heat is struck.

Stick Insect

Their eggs arrived in midchildhood, swapped
at school in tissue-filled matchboxes and
never hatched until they bled time under
our feet for estar is metalegged. You have
to stare through these words, their feelimbs to
see how in the leaflost eyeset's emboniments
they across the intimeless florever.
Now in thorn wornaments the mystery
shopper triggerfingers her undigits.
Making strange is the chisel she lifts to
chip sky away, leave skins like crisp-packets.
Absence tolls its bells inside her, and
magic pulls strings to which nothing
attaches. Attached to that nothing are
the black flowers, expending in the losts of time.
Daring to stand under the stars each week
the dream lessens the skeletons from
their leaves. Sleepwinds the contradiction
torn shadow-bank, dreamputated
anatomic menacles. The clash of
two nothings makes a kind of motion:
bluebell-tremble, shadode of blood is
the tree we uphold so that it may flower
in packed senses of malware. Then the car
alarms will sing to us in our states.

Harvestman

Stalking over the gas barbecue when I
unshroud it its body balances be
tween moments as a collector of shadows
through stone fields picks off windrows I am
shown how meanings cling in secret bodies
cadenced in those outliens of the dead.
A spidersplinter lunglost as ashheaps
the blown hairvest of scriptype
errorglyphs. It is found in illinear
camerangles that threadeye the ether
ways. Cornquistadors of the eggcase-
helm are eldoradoing to the farfuture
on antennable shimmerchinery. Their
strutlegs tarnish the nonentropic toraveller
in godments of musicoskeletal
duskguise thru saharanges that skirr
to selfloss. Thus the pholcid wobbleans
thitherworld. Scuttling the vestment
nights connect is a vacancy
in the mold thru which the moon caves
and gives me crumbs. Puppet, we cut
thereads that moved you, the queried leaf
is here to dissociate you howaver
you felt still shadows sleep at your foot,
steps akin to skin, thin figurations
asking your thoughts. Allelbowed terr or
fist hehesitate on the podium
apprehensile of wherevery spiderung
is thicketting to painstake.
Eitherway there will be no cost to you
the consumer, myth that you are,
slur of impulpable ego. Think that faster.

Chrysalis

Teleology has ended, tautology remains:
the sleeping child is in the sleeping bag.
This green casque outdoes elegance, has nothing
to wait for but flesh's remission; nor
does she void excrements, nor eat unless
moved as a kayaker through sapid canyons
betworlds, the one seeping, the other
resembles that not properly awake, yet
her arm in its sleeve shifts, when matter
cries in caves of albumen, in dense aspects
we replace stars by hand in red: start
from where we are not and climb from there to
tweentime, self-urge scars into prose as
she rises songless through dark pushes
perhaps smoke hears her tottery frame
untogether and nothung, the eyes of
the dead are ring-pulls and their content spares
her bracketted ears and mezuzah-scrolled
skin. Uturn about face all that is sullied:
erasure of margin, elision, phase-out that
sleeprids the creditroll. Grave imaggots
make falsidles, unlessen by unctuation
until pappy or permeaty. Inside is novel
made of armies clashing on television,
novel of ideas destroyed by the act of reading.
Beyond its meanings wrapt in white sameness
in rolypolymorphous peeving under
the fern's ribcage or deadleaf: she waits to tell
the future what the future cannot bear.

The Moths

I.

Once the moths had been twin rulers of the earth
along with their day-brothers the butterflies
although in fact the moths held primacy because
at this period most things happened in moonlight
and they were the bearers of souls' breaths.
There were legends written on the hills then,
and tainted substances of thought. When
a scale fell from a moth, stone happened, owls
screamed names of god as the forest winked.
In day-time the world slept and only
the butterflies went anywhere, among bluish
blush of bush or shrub, anthered paper
machines, unseeable illuminations. No one
noticed how they blinked their blackberry-
black eyes and plotted. Soon a belief started that
wings are an expression comparable between
species, and the moths then adorned themselves
but never approached the secret beauty
the butterflies candled to them, magnificent
in their richness, it was said, as the Tyrian.
In those days the sun was black and
about the size of an egg, few knew what it
was for. (When the first clouds had stormed love
it had come to nothing save this, issue of dust,
brainball). It hummed under its breath,
perhaps with sarcasm, or malice. A gang
of butterflies could smother it, they thought, not
knowing it was gravity's centre. Each with
one wing stuck they opened and closed
like fans, futilely, flypapered, massing
until the sun heaved with shuttering
wings. Then a moth flew up with an ember
at its ferntongue tip, and the butterflies

fireballed. Sun was now day-God.
From that time the moths would seek any light
but sun, while the free butterflies basked in
the solace their ancestors were, like kings.

II.

All it is is in its tricky construction,
a mathematical ghost
precisely not there
as it unleaves the trees

erring on the sides of error,
it dusts a door or silts over a wall

is nothing but that which the name
is full of like a leaf failing
to fall or a hand walking across a page

sense is held at arm's length

fettered to the lettered wings
it flattens on alighting.

Touch is to its palp a flex
nerve-ending its feel.
Ferntip of the tongue thing gone
spiral, gone fishing, done thirsting.

Cinnabar Moth

*As I stared at it, it seemed to speak in a small piping voice,
terrible small and thin, but terrible human.*

An angry crowd is one. Also
Mussolini pupating from a gantry:
all it is is in its tricky construction,
from its flatpack it struts itself out with
a tiny key for many hinged components.
Selfconstructs, eggs out limbs and
stalks the godark, collects
the baggages of adulthood
pumps into wing until nothing is faint
the ink is wet behind the trees
capillary tongue reversengineered
to suck the U out of the mouth,
to eyestalk an unlettered sentuntense.
Fettered to the wings it flattens
on alighting, gleants arguseyed, fastens.
Stop poor sonnet and resemble
me my face is strangely notlike
swear the eyes to secrecy and implore
the sugars to frostlace the flawflow
that the lost daughters of grass believe
the wind sleeps no god is without fire
cremation is creation otherwise,
the words inside the meat come
loose so punctuate the ragworthy flowers
new metals gleam in labgloved hands, they
take on our unexpressed senses,
chemishperic spell: touch
is nerve-ending. It leaves with the light.

Clothesmoth

Before and after dust there were no angels
so I made a nest against language.
It was a lung that breathed night, digested
keratin skin threadslicks and infringes.
In the eggtime of my gulagging
the slips of childhood bred understairs
where seemstresses assembly-lined smocks
who grew fingers out of sense, affraying at
the corners of me, furred like the dead I
believed in and cannot leave, stalked on the rope
in the mirror. By secret antipathies
I pulpitated in sleevelest. Floursome
foundress of the staircease: the instrument
hunted me and its tongue heavengendered
yet bred gladly in that evilair when
the night before's rain wovelength in the trunk,
its head written cloud, this was the sign of
rebellion in all angeldom to solve
old curtainties. Through all th'empyrean
down they fell. Lead forth my arméd Saints
by thousands by millions rang'd for fight;
nothing is less than named. Shadean
velveteaters rattling over the Caspian
intimeated the disinformed sky that
if there's anything left living bomb it.
The threat-level remained tense to breaking.
The pattern in the carpet is vomit.

Hawkmoth

I prise her apart and find inside her
the sun's photograph and names of sleep
since automatic days end in strokes,
spokesongs, downscales, the deep-
damasked mothself dies when the tree draws
happenless air to inhalations
and history prefigures in the mess
ages that are stars and clouds
successively obliterating each other
a crude synthesis timescaling
where rust self-references the wing.
Thorax hulked like a boeing fuselage.
Flip the belieflong logodesigner, to
puddle in the eveling for petrochems
a mouthroll tonguelolled its leafloose pilifers
as the felttipped moonslight uncrewed.
I spoke sleep as particles of night crashed,
a severed leaf broke through
the sky and the trisdust. It carried its
open letter to the gods in a puff
of sad. As I went to the toilet it
was heavy enough to cascade dust from
the lampshade, and its low hum reminded
me of one I took in a matchbox to
school, something wrong in its palpable mass.
This piece of darkness I circle as I
stab the lights away of a childhood whose
truth seems less than the moth. Dad, it was you.

Ant

I.

A foot under the paving is a sand lung.
Do not stand in the hatched area.
If blood trickles up, it
is ant, quickly individual,
arranged jointly, signing love.
The rain stays its hands for it, because
desert is only an act away.
The periods in the grass are moving,
their snap-together limbs spell
a word lugged in as seed,
release crumb or moon.

Their serif legs come to paragraphs
they cannot cross, and even
on a hand's interstate, they trot
as if on a familiar track
towards their lost telos, their
ends threaded on your palm. Shock
of the known, the noun.
Who can tell the answer from them?
They ground the earth to a stop
and form the lettered multitude,
columning into the earth
to store their limbs in holds.

Where dung raises the mushroom
they fold the mountain, raise a crust.
For one day, through the whole borough,
the bricks of the street-facing walls are
chocked and mica-shiny with wings.
Ascending updraughts, swifts and queens await.

II.

Canny askeletal question: each time an ant is lost, should you pay attention? It is as stray money, hair in bread, an individual word, snatch of speech. Once I found one crossing a page of my book as I read in the car as we submarined the Channel c/o Eurostar. Although moving, this ant was dead—it would never find the pheromone-trail back to its mother. The ant searching for its poem comes adrift when it crosses the noncrease knee, able to unwithstand the tide of information with clogged feet. I repressed an impulse: to drive home to release it onto the paving-stone-crack from whence it climbed. Being in a tunnel made me think how each spring tiny cones of dug-out clay are left outside our door. There is a city under the city. Deep in these holes they celebrate mass to embody the paving's stored energy. An antic epic archived in a deep incunabulum describes the finding of a discarded kebab. The same with words: find one lost and we have a duty to return it to language, and its nest-mother, the poem. But usually we leave the word as found, weighed down by calls upon the particular; the extended holiday of not writing. A discourse is another person's instrument, but in any bullet-point there is this pupal belonging, a smell-trail back through forests of grass to caves where the eggs are stacked against us. A city falls in the rain, the ants seize our grains. The tittled aristocrats are beheaded and restored as crowned unheads. Adjust the mot juste to get Saint-Just who dissembles to 'Ant is just.' The epic is poem plus ants. This which shelves between us can take human form, can in that pure light trapped under which the road is tunnel the ear, bearing a replica egg. The lost ants' broken syntax destroys roses. Unaimed and unnamed, the gyre loosens in the parabled corn or behind a handynasty vase. Humean billiard balls strike out to follow the hox gene down the orchard. Here we find spines and symmetry, then suddenly the ants drive upwards in force, shepherds from whom a sonnet will pipe. Nomad is neither island nor tending to dystrophy, in groups, singing hemichaunts, they are ascending to milk the stem-mothers. Poems sustain low-level weed-growth, fending off predatory antiselfs. If we reduce want we get ant. Reduce poverty to get poetry. Oppose the system, end up with antimperialism. The lost ant by Grimm's law changes to the lost chant which by Hart's rule becomes the last chance which by Murphy's law becomes loose change which by Kant's categorical imperative is given away which by the third law of thermodynamics is spent which by free association becomes spurt which by I-ching becomes sport which by the law of untended consequences led to an unabandoned shed in county Antrim which by the McNamara fallacy was bombed which by Stigler's law of eponymy reverts to Grimm which mutatis mutandis turns to poem which by mob rule unturns the urn, returned silence, burnt algorithm, antic and ontic ant, found word, émigré or emigrant.

III.

Once I found one circling on my table in a café, in March, divining a lost pheromone-trail under plates and among coffee-rings. I imagined a corridored world, under-ground, with no main thorough-fares. To get anywhere, to say arrive home, you have to choose between thousands of rooms, with doors leading to more, and each one has a slightly different quality, you pass through a thousand living-rooms to reach yours, where the light-bulb bares its filament for you alone. A drift is aliving in their sensing as the clock-work sleeps. Unidentifiable in their smallness they gather when our elegies are lost, we force them on the page but they fly like black birds back into the trees. Also once I saw one on the rim of the office toilet. Others I have seen word-riven, sword-lit, or sense-attacked, vending-machine illuminated in the wine-dark them-park or quishy among the fecundary homes, post nature. Dilatorily out-of-place, its tongue-wet rubber-end connected its cock-eye. Don't think straight think like the thread a rain-drop makes upon this window, the bread's breadth is dense with what procreates, child-head heaps up, in such situations, we describe a circle or my feet make a line not scan. The signified cannot hear the signifier, the road composes its waking life. I ran in the soul in the throat of the hour-glass to chance to be the fag-end in my own life-time. I have broke the folding eye and slept between the cracks protected by words, mere flames, lips crackling. There are silences lodged in hotels where we must trust the sentence to lead us before such a night as collapses in the smog, between the four chaosses contained in your loss. The eye-lash trembles under-hood, we have loved also a room the size of an eye where the imputed sky becomes plain, is aloof on the resting surface of arm, in here we feel or portray the silence we wish for as we sit behind the message that stirs in us, to share with the edge, for they say the ant's shoulder can carry away a house. The termite's man-high menhir foreshadows the mansion. In dactylic cling to wend the out-worn glossary its workings indentured in disrupts of shadow-stalk follow the proxied world-lord of lost river, ancient path, division of rain-drops, these follow no map, sweep before all in order to bear home the sugar-grain or an unchaperoned noun pounding from the broken hill of Europe. I walked past the table to a window, and a large balcony. There was a view of the lake at the bottom of the hill. It was blue, beautiful, and warm. No one was bathing there, the grassy shore clear, and the water translucent, inviting. Looking downwards things seemed full of warmth and potential joy, but I woke with a head-ache and a strong thirst. Chance fades like roses over them.

Soldier Ant

Smiting with an hammer in the garden at
rocks, they would be free of minutes.
Their call to arms might be
footfall, chemtrail, breadcrumb.
Upheavening in hostotality
they are looking for the bodies
they shriveled from. A joy-
tormented tumultitude of
centaurs in the dragonworld
sugarsurges to the spalatial chambers.
Political body is a panzer division.
Theirs is the world through which the writing
shows. When their army occupies
the dictionary, lawnforcement
breaks down to turf-wars.
When the Kings of Brazil are on the march
dismay is general, since they have all one soul
and make bridges of one another. River of
pureprose or chaingang. They cast stars as lots:
disorderers of seedstores, sappers,
deforesters of pages, agents of
entail, retail. In their khanates uzis
and calamiterrors spread heavy loss. Their cry:
allow the gods to judge men as you judge ants;
art is efflorescence of capital, no more.
Each fear handles its arms, swings warhammers
to make the sky stop then setfeet into
Noigandres and bladestorm the foodreserves.
The black-helmeted 6th foot charges into
the teeth of danger, it's said, to innovate
is to destroy the words fall wrong, cutting-
edge is cornquest, avant is guarded,
will not withstand the pincer-move, the drowned fields
of Mars where grass is flesh and art is dead.

Wood Ant

A future was forming under the needles.
We walked passim in sandals to the grey pile.
Roots flickered underfoot, parallel door
to innerworld, to shed a negative light,
to greet with the cast iron violences
of welcome, the self-got eggs forest-
ored within the stateletted small arms we
proked with sticks to see the firecrew manifest
crowd-agitation, spermen securitizing,
the formicable blackandecker start.
Wit's end is endnessless of the worknet
that nights will outnumber. Inutile
reality-claims are registered, in
columns wishes are washed away and rivers
torn between our hands. The poem kept
losing its face, the birds ate the path back
home. Re: Gretel, we missed the candyhouse
when Baba Yaga's shack stalked to Babi
Yar. wooded canyon of the old woman.
The wrong path having been taken when
Turkic nomads split or spilt westwards.
Language is to blame because it names things
and led little Hans to the oven door.
Where were killed so many I that my
feet were not full was one of these,
danced out of the seams. The pliered meat
leant inside and senses congregated here
to prave the road to hell. The riverice
broke, the trees judged. A trickle of picnic
stricken tray dippers escaped, this way,
quickly, remember our parents for
easting in earths. They already foreget us.

Wasps

I.

For days I have watched them
in their roadmender jackets
heads to the wall, airborne and air-born,
threading a crack, touch-feeling
a route into the ventilation grille.
One evening I puff a cloud inside.

When I look next day, their house
is made of paper, brain
cased snugly in the wall-void.
Their bodies parked, as if in
a port of delicate craft, after
a sandstorm, or as if touched
by sleep, the dust they folded under.

I brush away the poison
and unhang the paper lantern
and as I hold it a breath of wind
blows its roof away to show
its inner tissues, the pupae
responding inside their cells
like baby's fingers.
I call my son to see this—
this stillborn blindness that will not live
and he tells me to put it away.

Standing with him in the sun
this white powder coming down on us
is only sunlight, through puffs of cloud.
But those grubby digits he had seen
reached towards the light we stood between.

II.

Weaponise the intelligentsia.
Have complicated mouths that
cluster appleception's semimetaphor
and faces as do machines.
Trapped with beltlet and epaulet
afflicts of the goldammed angerangel
airsense the vortical sculvert in
chemtrails of currency-manipulation
to police the subhubbubs of underskull:
out of newspap's prosingsongs
to malaxate a shardy lapalace.
Disfruit the fervourite armamask
underhand a sinewavy transmutter.
Grate heads on glass. Flame-tune the
mouthparts. When they find the cure
for poetry, it will be 7 parts wasp.
Raptor at the aperture, sawer of law
where the tree earths its stone
relinquash that palpapple ecomerz
hesitate ferever on the word for
this fuhrious buzz from the jaw
hewn summer-palace, harmlet's home.
For ages it suffered forage-rage.
Forages it suffered for age-rage.
Interwinter with us, compound in
the dadorail. We shall not know
or kill you until in spring you jetlag
down the curtain with the worst hang
over, cling loggily to the waste-basket's
rim, and reviving in the warmth of my hand
assume the posture of a told-off dog.

III.

Maotsetung checks in to Schlosch Malebolge.
A ghost dips in the crystal its image of
desensed head hanging from the crossbeam
as burn-victims are inverted to facilitate
blood-flow. His mouth shoots semi-autonomous
drones among the applefall, the fly zone.
These ground to air bullets are thoughts.
The nursery is ideaswarm, peer inside:
nightscrapes the glare-winged window-
wing fanning with cellophane. In the Head
Archive dossiers are chewed over, in the
infirmary ans are added to aesthetic
technicians draw the screen so silently.
His thoughts are tending the Elysee's wide
grounds' smoking orchards. The peace process
is ongoing. Conference of worms, of flesh,
comes to its predatormind outcome. Swarms
blue the horizon, the media plants in
the archival mudflat its cuneiforms
concerting the busy griefs. Playing queen save
the god in puckfist of clamber-music
the delegates over dinner speak
meatlanguage of force majeur, tongueglue
the inabrogable protocols. They don't
say how each war is ground for the next: bombs
are eggs of grubby dormant dynasties.
We once incolouded their briefest discourse
saw in their paper, to spit through the gagged
dumb-mask the weaponry weeps and feasts.
Powersurge blows the chandeliers.
Thought, only nature can destroy the state.

Hornet

Dumb money made a world called work.
Work opened its capacious door
down which gorge music lapped.
Each wingscaled spinetip nest
egged the incanaveral vespid
bioaccumulated morphologies as
hyrnetu, hernet, harnette, hornette.
Civic oventrance beclame a nocument
of trumpetry. Muscularm the word-
swordman's stormstress to whir a wingbeat in
side me as hourglass-shaped time. Eric
Thorax's thistlewords are thwack and thwarm.
Let me intrude myself. My swordlit
wordlist is unchanted to meet you, I
spent summer wrenching apart quotation
marks with the pair of my hand the hair on
my tongue. I tunnel eyes, yolk headlesions.
The trees do not fit so I replace the
alphabet carefully. The mood of
the light walks in and saturates, as
a rain with name. A sky leans open or
the smoke unrests on the roads in panic
hum. In a pale woman's sunglasses I
see my fear, pack iron, infer history
is held together by her anotherness.

Ichneumon

Sumer is icumen
are the children all in bed
the wormonger is sawstruck
by hypoderm of demi-sheath
she feghteth nat gladli wt ye serpent
& to unnerve the worm
embeds a broodthirsty jaberror
or arrowslits a crockadrill.
The misuscular bride, she arms her
telescopiform eggtube leavalives
the surgical target-grub, its pinhead
impregnate severybody
with a heatseaking stickin
jection. Her hourglass-
waisted secuitry of motherlove
since the unnameable cry in the night
with unaccountable eyes is hers
until enemerges the unembodied pulpoet,
wedgemarking the tablets that de
sign the adobedaubed hovel's
ventinlet. The analytical engines of
the line emusculate the bodymelt
to eyejack the hostess, hearteaten
nature is telephoning us in sleep
to say. Sumer is no more.

Caterpillar

Someone whispered to us something gentle
in the night that we don't have to think
about, just know: or we ganged upon the rose
hiding under the petal to the ends of the eye
while the finger of the state pointed:
do not operate among his furnaces: the birds'
breaths hardened and in that steam grew
famine of bread and great cleanness of teeth:
the skeleton rattled in the leaf underfeet
the materials accordionfolded as bristled
eyebrow came down the unrose to touch
the sphinx's anal horn: that tonguefelt moonrind
as slow bombs hatched in hedge
rows: pale antlers reminded us of our mother's
grief: we gaubed with our treaded feet: to wield
logic: the nipplegged
unsides as a blow to ribbons, towards
the withering of scale: percepts yielded to fog-
disowned imagos who lunched upon
vegetation's stripeaten constructs
of labortheory: sun-comprehended
we hungermarched the ribbitten leafstems,
hobnailed from here to timesend, distend,
rasping text, cutting windows
so the slow vivid leaves canceled one at a
time. In our membrainy midgetsuits we
sang with insinuous accordiong
constructed a sentence to hang from,
secreted sense, talked spin. Scorolled
our prolegs in chimeratic leaftime
to chrysalistize dearthread from
the cremaster, mistwisting in pupation.
Coddled in a genizah mortuary
our streams sought a source. The eye roots,
bones store night. Each motherson must debody
by shiftwork the chenille of disunction, the leaf.

Inchworm

The poem opens with four great metaphors:
I am your team-manager, inchspector,
the gibbetted emperor of emptiness
I parasail onto your shoulder and mostly
you do not notice me fuddling. It's late:
the moon is shrink-wrapped,
a car bends a shadow round us.
You turn, a tree leans confidentially
ducks cluster and the falling leaves look like
money. At the end of each apple a tree
pulls back: a road travels from the tree
through the words. Statistical engines are
climbing towards us to foretell a new suit
to measure capital unhead the hand
a gleam of now along the carpet or
a small tunnel under the road
culverts a stream away. Together
we'll leave no twig unmeasured
yardstick the wormslengths the metric
intolerance things have, the shape
we come to call name: no ideas but
inthings, no idea who parted the
weather from its earth, nothing but
the inventions of the past. The book reads
evening is a dim passage along which
obstacles gather. A small leaf is edged with
it as a shadow falls from a plane
and a hinge closes between clouds.
Geometry halves into a dance of fragments:
that monolith of letter, protractor
of silences, accords sensation to the dead.

Butterfly

My son picks one up, balls his fist
and lets it fall, a sweetwrapper,
a flap, its eyelined hindwing stopped.
I think of sugarseeking fissiles,
brides striped bare, animate flowers,
emberesses of reinsurrection, tongue
trumpets, smutches on the theomorph,
shieldbearing foldolks, flutterances
of mimicrism, incoils of noonsense
or self-adjusting flames when
a dream unfinishes. It is time for such
sundrugged cloudware to uncoil nozzles
and betongue the frostrotted materfall.
Somewhere, someone makes a violin
laugh. The humankind hands of gods
leak from their skies as she puts
out her eggs like milkbottles.
Thewing is a page on which
an image nights its twist in wind,
an edge where child can be put
firm in his bed as the word in the mind,
the pharmaceutic scent-tuft spinoffs
and gatefold tensions the nosefeeds,
tissued looseleafs, riffles the pages
to take leave of your fences.

Cabbage White

Twice that day I saw paired cabbage-
whites dancing together: once by the beach car
park while loading the children and then a hundred
and more miles later where the hedge of our garden
ends, unloading them, and it was hard not
to see them as the same pair, after so
many clouds had slipped over the windscreen,
dancing in alternature. Days then
were what dreams ordered, appearing in
an old movie where they speak funny enough
for you to feel the language-change, where
it is rainng the past, the face, sides, echoes,
it is raining ideology. Inside our
houses are inner ears. With them we fill
our never-ending nerve-ends with the speeches

of that which surrounds. Hear me then when I

say Where death comes to the egg, the nymph,
is that spurion we need to complete
the calculation: each query comes with
a person attached: the ghost of a machine
releasing eggs tonguetwisted the timesoil
the newborn bones piled where the dance
began as the water spoke of doing, we read what
the printer deathrattled, or we could be
pinned to moons to fan the beams from her
sleeping eyes, look how she scatters
eggs through space and time to reduce
predation, the past gets paster whose sun
is a photographer whose flash lasts all day
where a tongue curled in fern unfinished, slipping
into evening, the children hit sleep.

A watchmaker looked with distaste at the
stiff processes of ordinary machinery and
sought with a wrought butterfly to imitate
nature, fluttered this forth that lit on my finger's
tip and set its gold-speckled wings, as if
in prelude to flight. The rich down
was visible upon its wings; the luster of its eyes
was instinct with a spirit softened in
to this ideal-realized butterfly; not
among faded earthly flowers, but
those which hover the media of paradise
for the spirits of the unburied infants
to disport themselves with. From teepeed
eggs the thin caterpillars uncoiled,
swept in wet flush under closed birch

canopy each traceried flowerburst spread

under the ivyvine-veined pylons
the deranged wall, the healed field
when the life you bled turned the book
of five corners, and trees printed the tractatus
of spring before the candle held still the giddy
stars with their one idea to give tongue
to the languageless lands with precision
disengaged from the pistil the whey-thief
wheeled then and sate upon these tornopenings
her eyes faded me like a white piece
of rigid satin cloth stirred thither
in the night. A pale petal has left the flower.
It unblinks like a shutter on a dead-
small camera: the picture it takes is
itself. Dew-wet weed of dawn, adieu.

The Earwigs

I.

There is an afterlife for dead religions
in books, leafed tenderly by divines,
and every few years a horny earwig
climbing the hollow of a spine will
leave its shit-offering, the size of
a full-stop. It walks languages into
the carpet, knows the ant-entrance to
the paving-stones and waits outside

as out of the plane-pierced clouds step
the ancestors, their feet sticky
with discharge. In their stale corridors
their carapaces have lustre

and smell of underground carparks
where leaves roll themselves into cartridge
flowers undo their colours
and the deleting angel
opens a drain to the roots of the dead.

Such massed silences here in the eye,
its cartilage globing the hole
night pours into; hard of smell, the shell
opens in the drain, stink wakens
in fridge-fringed work-spaces.

When the explorers force their way into
the moss-forest's phosphorescence
they are pieced apart by pitch-
forked splinters from this underworld,
and their pinches can not wake them.

II.

Ultipurpose toolkit includes
folktongued forknife, pitchfork-prong,
metafork sandmother of the nemesystem,
dung-fork, twitch-ballock twincers
forceps, gutwrench, treefold
to tip the scale, Octeon Plus (56xx) processor
at up to 600 mhz with 8, 10 or 12 cores
supporting 1) line monitoring for routing
& traffic capture through front panel
10 sfp+ interfaces 2) passthrough mode
with a single 10 ge module and a xaui connection
3) protocol & security offload by processing
trafficstreams entering or leaving the platform
4) toolkits such as 6windGate for embedded
networking its witcharm in rockabides
subhub lilty aeligature of the swamp
weremember, earwugger, spork
for feasting in crawlspaces
and unendulating remains to the next shadow.
To the scrumping isolater the apple
opens its cavern inside which awaits
the tree, attached to my silence you said
from inside the stone lungdust
and darkfold the demiurgent mirrordoor.
Hithither it illfeels a manmangled
selfroot a shopsoiled remembrain,
voice still trapped in the stone.
A piece of me comes loose and opens
the door, there is a self at the end of the
finger, in the slept dust, the point from which
the whale from the floorboards surfaces.

Bees

The architect builds the cell in his mind before he constructs it in wax.

I.

The ratified bees, the governmental bee.
The identical bee crumbles from
its hiventity, its eyes
speculate in the compound sun

plentiful form of self is storm,
an eye which tracks a hand's
thousanding fingers, unsound
the hair is crawling with noise

or just crawling, warmswarm
it armlifts an air, airlifts
its warm arm, legs the breeze, hums
like one pretending to helicopter

they commute like us, not by helicopter
by willpower, season-ticketed, from
the roof-straps of invisible trains.

Later in the day you'll see them
leaning like car-mechanics, or actually
old-fashioned fat pump-attendants.
One will check your oil by pushing
his body deep under the hood
inserting a long nozzle; to whom
you, the driver, hand cash and then see
his unshaved, oilslicked face.

These are their textures: of elated flowers, of
data fogs in a light understood rain,
of a numerous god named hum,
of the tongues with which we'll see.

II.

Aftersleep in our pinholed shells
we're speed or seed cameras,
pursuing a faint ascent over
the programmed grass where
are those age-old golds
the mountains whethering
and music fragmenting ahead

the songs in us sweep down loud
canyons and stack in flower-
heads of willow-herb leaning
hard on the untwined song
chief among us is one who dances
a name around corners,

run of the million the plant-planets
explode language, each one a new

understanding of the rain to
make a rope and make a fist,

we tangle into thirstless thistles,
its mud-bronze weaponry
flow coldswarms, warmscolds

each of us a furlined pilot in helicopters
the naked eye makes invisible

on the flower's ironwork landing-platform
we extend our feeding nozzles and get
a free paint job thrown in
then knock down the sky, one word at a time.

III.

Touch the rail, dust clings to the finger-end.
The glacial moon stamps on the sill,
gold drags her eyes into the house
of money, to the deposit of life's rich hours
wage-laboured lines cross this water-stain
moraine, with hoover's cyclone freeing Ötzi
from lint, ginger-tufted cadaver with
leathern tinder-pouch: his days of honey
tongued forages swept into downswing of
coagula after icemelt the clung
pollen dates the goldenmost naufrage of
crystalleyed dissembly into knees, pins,
membrained caramels of palearctic
disarticulation. Glacier's tongue retracts.
Lodged in a deadpan dustentangled
as England, as couplets, as elegy for tea.
Hexameter's alluvium is inchscaped
in imargination as if we slip in sleep
and cannot quite recover each object
in their selfless pursuits of gravity:
✔disposable hooverbag as chambered tomb—
✔iceage succession as day/night—
✔bee's knees as in mind your own. Own your mind—
✔death as lost data. Rail against rail.
The clotheared mothman in guise of
railway suicide in striped overalls
bristles crimescenery's counterscape
as behooves the walrustusked shipwreck
because manmoth be he-moth to she-bee
deadscrolled for urnburial at sea
barked of tongue's sunchild until that head rots
and a new one rises out of time-pieced
DNA, soul's cellmate and self's soulmate.
Disembodily seedeyed the emptied
reliquary lies. Boombusted, sensate
or napping, fat comedian of the letter be.

IV.

At assembly the head's speech
is interrupted by dancing implying
the engine is the angel that wiring
is wrong in the face. The birds execute
sound-values through a window
as sealed against winter thumbs of us
come between the air, the hatched
machine-gaze in each cell codes
across its stem-language spines,
particularities, each time the arc
of the hive wakes, in its interests
we touch-type the uneconomic
data of honey-rust, a waxed
codex explains away capital flights.
We must treat the past tenderly, as
librarians redress piperolls, secrete
in them the sucroses of experience.
Constructs of dream abuzz
the threading afternoon, the hand-trees
wave, our screwy tongues have grace when felt
gleams fertilize its statue and statue
gleams, horizon is a line of a poem
that broadly does not mean what it says, the birds
must be mistaken, earlily crowding
an empty platform. The wave is ill.
People drive their boxes towards us,
listening to great music. Their heads take
time to reach us as with or without
body matter attracts souls. We seed
by exploring, that stamen waits in an ice
cream realm to unpipe music, extrude
beard, apply government like make-up, with
fogged souls form an association of rain.

Bumblebee

Our lawes are like to a Spyders web, which the Humble Bée doeth break and rush through at pleasure, but the little weake and small flyes are catchte therein.

The things that name themselves are few.
The baronial anthologer unbuttons his eyes
comfortumbles the bellybeard
mandibbles the probeable hairim
from his mitey timeship patches a feedthrough to
the Public. He trembles a tormental trimbone
& bebops hegarmonies of nonsonsong
disarms thistles, tilts the lavender shoot
tinaturns between the roses,
plumps and circumchances, has
a rough-maned clamber on the parapetal
flowerring to mumble on gasmasked
calls for an earial bombeardment.
He breaks the law and the law winds.
On the meadow's wide battleground he pur
sues the fire-fangled dandelion, jaws
open for pollen. Sky makes stuff for him to sing.
Rain falls on his manes, the Virgil
fragments he picked up in the rain
wait for judgement. Sunsets describe a turn
in the wheel, the gilled mushroom broadcasts
invisibly as god translates the flowers
tending to dogends and ovengloved purseloins.
Jets burn like cigarettes, their wings
tender. Brushstrokes of the sipway
leaflitter scentdances through the field
spreading pollen over their dresses
eyes filming the evenings before this when
the felt clock made boot upon the summer's velvet.

Honeybee

We are humsandbeings
carrying language's language, long
hauled from distant blooms
to the house that name built.
Round here no one calls it poetry.
We dance like a numerous god
like purseloined prefugees
from a word that has not been thought.
Our achtongue tralalanguage
from farfurlineages of humdrome
dipthrongs a hexagone incomb
in zoosemiotic mittenish, singlanguage.
The planes are stacking up as
we swarmturn and flowerfollow
the wax-pocket and pollen-basket
enacting a sentdance as lingua estinta
rotates against us. What bleeds across
lawn is dark. We are mindful
of pastendustrial seminature
odeing into this hole that
closes when the lid fists
the angels ungelling until fungus
splits from our seams.

Flea

Cancel my subscription to *The Fleaiad*, to *Pulex*, to
Ad un pulce sul petto di B D, to *La Bottega de Chiribizzi*,
to *Cuartets en loor de la pulga*, to *Suplicio
de un piojo cogido en fragrante delito*, to
Capitolo del Pulice, to *La Puce de Madame des Roche*,
to the thought that all leaves are full
of worms and those worms are possessed with
spirits, that they leap and skip in that brief concept,
to the dream as a face to the head to be seed
of destruction, to Mother Fluxus, to transgressors
of scale, debtors of our unurned outcomes, to Poetry,
to Hopkins and his hopkind, to the poet
who rhymed Goethe with teeth: we once were
part of the hatch now sit in idle fires and wish
the wings back on the page,
*atomo viviente entre los pechos blancos de
Leonora hermosa, aquellos bellos miembros
delicados: al expirar la pulga dijo ay triste.*
To Hill the latinate, to Prynne the indo-
European roots. Haunted by the unconceived
children of relationships that consisted of
no more than a few words, a glance
along a crowded train-carriage and come out
like a coin from the clean hand of a magician.
*Ainsi petite Pucette Ainsi Puce pucelette
tu volettes a taton Vueillez o dieux que je tombe
sous un si noble tombe au milieu des deux mamelles.*
Askewer of the leapt telescape swells
with one blood made of two: it sucked me first
and now sucks the juice of word, the milk
of parodies leapt from me who surfet
on your peachy breast, were I he I would not
bite you but search some other way to delight
you, never die for that drop's sake which he sucked
from your vein adjust your bra to give him room
or let your ivory nail prepare his tomb. To *Time*, to *Life*.

II.

Bombvoyage, headgeared hopkin
gone to heatseek the undivisible
imalcule in genergy's decreepit
doglegend, via underarmbitious
cattailists and rateaten disbodies,
plying the coatline from col to toeclip.
Exspokesman for bebop, monadminded
auger of oilepoch, teleconferencing
in your midst, hist the wind,
grit out lovesongs on a toy guitar.
Establish your wellhead then upheave
bloodsoil. Unhear a rustslur that tiptups
plaguevector: abandon all hop
fulcrum a nonsensable scale
on wareconomy paper
as inaudible violins play concertos
of the pester-marketer and pirasate.
Farfling the woundword
in lovelocity, its kerflop
manifeasts on the mountinfinite.
In the intricate hour, what is invisible
coats us, and is not found, and is not lost.

Caddis

In the slough of trough the rough of sough
in the silence the river seeped a self,
pools spooled their ropes to recreate
the Enigma of Isadore Ducasse.
Compassion was over again.
My jellies subset, I fell as leap.
There was a case that world encased,
that a stone sobbed to dream itself
harder. From dismay to dismember
this imputee's cladded head snorkelled the
timesheats. I caulked my archaic torso
bivvy-bagged in shadowash or
opened a door in mud bathrobed
as longtheriver the tanged and tined
processed by barge of state,
tubed hornpipes partuttered
shallow-shanties, laid hornpipes.
You will be cured they sang, in
the time it takes the fossils to swim
away, then meltamorphed into
a malevolice quire to foldoverol
the page of day songcycled that
tocometime is suturesque, involves
stilldeath in the stickleblack headhatch
where glovends of incunabulus are brawn
to the netherword in protolith.
They shadowdrowned their sursuits not
thinking of ziplocked corpse as depth-charge.

Leatherjacket

Everyone seemed to agree this part of
the poem was great. I had no memory
of writing it and read it over be-
bemusedly because the second page was
smeared with paint, the part where I describe
how we learn about fear through sleep, how
the tonedeaf stone takes pains, makes ways into
clades as a word lists it is time to glamp
in sadomechanical gimp gear
winkle-tight as God the chlorophyll out
sells / excels his leaf and to this our
unformed lives cling, as carefully
made ruins of poems are ploughed to dust.
The ear stalks what spends the night with
wheat reckons the seeds, we are all we
contain, sunlight hung across a web, nights
shining under the tomb. When hard and soft
interact is when things encapsulate
in membrane, egg, or seed. By grace of sun
we'll fasten Jimmy Dean in kneelength
trenchcoat nature-identical with rearvision
as the wind rushes the mirror's window
into the past we nostalgize the biker-
gangs, the bunches of wild, the cool shades who
climb out scathed in slut-bellied jackets,
enacting birth-myth with cartouched hair
because animal is future ash, untold ruins
await the telling, the told. Cornmother
to corndoll, cornhusk. All we see
of anything, side, angles, eyemelts.
The long walk to return the eggs begins.

Bot

Being time, this is my skin bullet, composed of rings with a double set of chiselteeth, undercarriage furnished with hooks, for taking hold of an inner coat, o the shadow bursts from inside. Here it spends the winter, and at the pouring forth of sun when it is an inch long, it disengages, and being carried through the intestines, burrows in the glowth; and changes into an oval black pupa with spiny amputands, from which, in some weeks, the perfect person sitting across from you is empty like a little tin pot. His name's Pol Pot, he hurt a lot, distressing it by the annoyance which it gives in the whitish crown of the head, the thorax black, retractile within one another; by means of this organ a hole is pierced in an ox's hide, the fly in depositing her egg, not that the stalked nights have openings for you. Cattle exhibit excitement and rush about, quicklips stretched forward, tails out, feeding upon juices beneath the skin, forming a sac within which it grows amid purulent matter suited to its appetite; and from which it unmuzzles its further transformations. Blades appeared that tense the humisphere. It is of a grayish colour, with large head and yellow face, and is most abundant in damp woody distracts. Sheep exhibit alarm when it approaches them, and seem to seek, by throbbing their noses to the ground, and by incessant motion of feet, to keep it from their nostrils. Ungum the moon, polish it so in the land where sand is kin to cloud the animals run thither, snorting. The common saying, that a whimsical person is maggoty, or has maggots in his walmart, perhaps arose from the freaks the sheep exhibit when infested by bots. Seek the warble: also warbot, escarbot. We are insists applying rain to the fingers we have buzzed out of the sluices of scartissue. It is in the floundress of the sheep that this fly selfseals, and the lipletters, when hatched, make their way into sinuses, I found movement under my skin since overtaken on the tongue's slipway feeding upon the juices, until they are ready to change to betterflies, when they find their way through the nostrils. These larvae move with dirigibility, holding by mouthhooks, contracting and elongating following regurges into an abstract of rosebud lullabides. Long-running shells and daemons reap the childprocesses. When noonstruck the sweatlicker heatsecrets unnature and ungorges the wordfall. In this case, misundersunder is a superterranean partmutter. New obfuscation tools enabled hackers to bypass detection by antimalware 27% of datamounts ripped searchbots in zero-day exploits 14% of organizations experienced a user downloading malware with torrents, anonymizers, peer-to-peer sharing used every nine minutes to combat other forms of bot-driven crime such as man-in-the-browser and automated Denial of Service 22% of digital display advertising traffic worldwide is botdriven exploited vulnerabilities including Apache Struts, Tomcat and Elasticsearch the infected system contacts a remote host via selfupdating features the command-and-control centers for the payloads are located in Asia every 49 minutes sensitive data is exfiltrated via configuration vulnerabilities 1% was controlled by a computer model of the basal ganglia 3% of adware was gubernational or antenational 48% of crypters had downtime errors in their rootkits 13% of end-users keylogged movemental vulnerabilities when circumventing the backdoor worm or toxing the popup trojanware 99% were vulnerable, hid themselves, their faces.

Maggot

History makes rubble and us.
Each morning the sheet I turn over
reveals a grub, impaled,
stemform of ponzischeme
where music is some fragment
that makes transition possible
so golisten the imagitation's
agog for applecaves of
luncheon on spewnaper, in
dugouts the harpeyed pulpalps
are nothing the inthing, to
meaternity's intraction
in phantom pleasure or
substantial presence in
bread's turnkinding. Beat
the heart of your community
malarveling in a gamutty longagog
that fruitwounds the tickeye.
Gogather tripent with a pieflip
hiroshimation's shemonster
selfmakes and flytips the child in white blood
who skulks like bodyhair of the planet
through the senseless apparatus of eye.
If you live in a house made of thought
or athwart the back-heart
the sun snubs and we gesticulate tears
or come reckoning as beaten songs
that stalk where the queen
rots in state, seseeding
the sows of her own construction.

Grub

Ich, ich, tissue of flies, speak. Lay claim
to the pay clay, newsfeed from selfabsorbing
silkeye your broodcast of morphous
polyversity. We struggle hardly. We
hardly struggle. Feed us on hides so we
fit inside the rain lotting the increments
to their places. Gothrough the meat that
contains us, we work to stop it rotting,
dislimbing the subsleep withinside
ensigngines since we pineyed the runsize.
The clock, storehouse of empty-headed crowns,
has designs, extrudes plans. Our mother
sun rises against us when the food picks
from the table it spells a city in which
screens aflight the cherubbed farfather the
unuttered purpulation of puposes.
Strong light spreads confusion the
russetting applerapture sugarsurges
under us to unhinge a rusting foodfoot
is a world bred of the nature of slime
& in maner as a snail tides on the paving
godfills the privy flypit the soulmotional
screameat surgests the mechasm
there is a mist in the heart of a country
we cannot appear to name. Our soft
infridged tripe is pure-rayed misuscle
the hemergent ununiverse as
pearversion of the underserved.
We keep the floor clean with our mouths
silvering sidelongly past the body
the song is lost to metre here rainbowpeel
heads roll an apple ripens in the heap
the ghost operates where the sentence transmits.

Nymph

I.

The remote would not work, or it was
lost in the packaging we build children
from, the ghosts sang illiquidity
a massive cloud penetrated the eye
forgegot an F-holed falset, the tine
of the year dumbfound the turn of the time,
crushed a gutterfly against the seem—
in the months to go before the war
against the hill, exhaustion ran from
your face as the fixed stare at the tea
cup's break where flowers made their mistakes.
Imagine a Dean or Phoenix at pond
bottom age-hardening until one night ready
to climb the reed to assuage their infancy:
mudlink water to earth, fengendered
branchildren fix idea on the leaf as when
each plane's shadow blinked instars of song
that force through the fuse a post-eco-
disaster blues, took place in our firing
aloft like the rose and in the film the slow
flakes of fake snow arrested in their falls,
the stars stuttered. All theories are wrong. Who
can tell the cancer from the cancan.
Amputands of candleblow felt mirage-rage.
Each ladder groaned under love, sped the word,
reasoned ways into tree, car, folded for
the mountains and mapped the sun. One day
they'll ride to the rose-lake dawns, luggaging
sideswayed by threadwidth to the birthstill,
damsel in dust dress askewing.
The villains are tired, they are spelt wrong.
Unfettered from your scubaqual forms
climb, clean-limbed, extrude, fly freely, and die.

II.

So much deepends upon
the waterflaw, the fathomable
corridor leading to inundraining
mirrodors where visectors ply among
seamonstresses whose throats
thoughtquench fry lifelong to
be mirrimaged by infantable simulars.
Namething bogsnorkels to airboretums
of boneloss with uboat breatholes.
The poem is nine parts water, one part life, is
phenomenal pond: by weight of time
the soulfisher stores mountains in eyes
wherewither to greensleeve untermenschens
of immortality. This is the irreversability of
exchange. Where you live has not
been told. My eyes liken
an aching future state is not responsible
for, and from the Pond of Despond
a black metaphor climbs. Waiting
for rupture it sets off in our words
for the shores of after. It is full of the eyes
in you, it wings from its name into song.
The hole it crawls out of was named the sun.

Oak Gall

I keep thinking about the gall
we found under the oak tree.
I told you there was
a worm inside and you

didn't believe me,
and was more interested
in splashing puddles
so that the mud varicose

veined your sparkly Barbie wellies.
When we got home I
sliced it with a kitchen knife.
At its core there was an amber

chamber that contained
a white grub, stirring, pin-eyed,
feeling
for the close walls it had been

slowly been eating out.
You looked for a second
and turned away and I held
the two halves together.

Bluebottle

Blubber your syllabilly tremblone,
betatest dreams above your workstation.
I shall spend my next five days
letting light lose itself inside a screen
neuromarketing an ingestments portfolio
until a piece of me opens and images
exit as from a headwound.
If the air spoke inwordly
nobode of the deathsent is
murmurmuring into an eartomb's
elevensing to milkclot the governmeat.
Listem the striplit signsongs
the cleptoparasite sups, ushers, shushes
upon gluts of ingotten illgots.
Crystaleyed the wind somewho
flows like a house at night and creates
wordslengths, casts silence and nightblooms
inside longunsung songs we understand.
Children cloud round us and from some
where an animal is still sobbing:
it so much wants to be human, to
build a house that is sentence, the wind
sticking to us the names of things.
If our eyes break open weight of dayness
we accentuate the apple-bowl's occupant
its blue-green shiny back sickens
into the song the illness of words.

Daddy Longlegs

Broken they show inside a kind of buttery filling, as if all along their roboticality was only on the outside, they were not after all mechanisms but soft things with flows and runs of sense. But this only applies to the larger insects, in smaller ones the liquidity is no more than a smear, that can hardly, I thought, speak of animality. Each awn wants, to feel is to ride the sentence out where in the dust limbs strut and tent on a typestract at x ideas-per-second. I considered how a windshield's star-crack is already bug-red, gunshot-holed. A scrapmetal spectre, wrought by fingers of air, one of its regional names was 'pull-the-legs from me'. I slept a fragment, how the hungry mirrors have the voice of the ocean, but never utter a sound. The glove of me is lost in upflows to self, lost in a crowd the great life-poem that writes its knowledge, the flaps of me in trees caught the blind light of the stars when the clouds impersonate dreams and aerial drones divetail the eyes' extent. I had crashed through so many ceilings that night and never yet grounded. Where the path's pith unsticks on their varnished lawns shone the vertebrate moon. The birds' empty empire aggregates poppy-appeals of overflights, Daddy looks blindly, a flashlit pullaway. Its abdomen oviposits sunward, tensingly. Speak stars, feel is what the head branches, intricate your forklegs, gristle etherness overthereal increation to suture a tonguentangled stumble ungainlily wingopening your fugelage as under the lamppost a bush holds in place a swarm of leaves. Farfeel from this to the midream of subterfuse, with eyetouch meander a circle of mist where stands your affable urchenemy: hell-bent drone, radio-silent and combat-ready. Disguised as pubic hair, walls have them: weeping-places, empires. Max Muller meets Max Miller. Once when you whirlwinged and danceforthed with a trembleast's zerosity we pulled your sandpitty knee-pans. Flameturned you to frailure and stink. Smeeched you to observe your *articulo mortis*. Allegged levitator, forgive us! continue please to carry us consternations, delations. Cling still to our interiors. Astronoughts and cosmonoughts, with tinyeared creaks above floats an angled sitar, we infotain the misses as we feel ash sifting, cloud's cellophane sealing us. Speak, stars, glutter tombfeelery's angulage, crashtest your skeletonnage-attachments against windows untilbody has pileupped the bonestar. Senseassult cloudware's suzerainty and doppelgang until undisentanglable and widespread into becomets.

You root the birds from their speech or fields entail their worlds between foxes. Suspended in daylight a grab floats. It is what spiders mean when they touch. The rain is on your side, on your front, the moon's inherent in the tenuous hold a mirror has, inside it still exists a population of captured ghosts. Then inwind blows and stars' strata of light and epiphenomenal jellyfish from which the flesh has weathered tangle in datasets. She pleads in lampplight for this to come untrue "I feel like a flailer, like languages colliding in space". she sputnicks where uniflied themory posits a loop loosening and air carries sentence-structures from her ashed face, latent as petalseed. Dance disasterly upon a pin, in the tanglage of langwidth. Breakleg the ogre-ego of languargue, manylegends are crutching towards us. Swallorswifts grey-out your ganglionic stiltstands as giacometrical disqualities selflossed when you semiskim the pondedges. The rain lifts from the city with the sound of the glassmen coming in the weakening sense of the sky. The clouds we like are made of this: expensive ships delicate enough to glisten. The streetlights dance for you and the tree does its appearing trick. There are seeds approaching. Antler into the bedroom then down stairs strut, crutch to the wall skreek Ah ash, set me ashore, return my legs.

Dragonfly

Suspend the alphabet
bushes curve in the manner of music
the flowers sing: an adderbolt
wingtips, has struts and frets
with hakenkreuz fasces
metalarmed in icarush of sunsation.
The film the sky plays is null without this
we walk to where they are in shot
freezeframe these archenchantresses.
A mirriage of scarpmetal heatrays
the fairytailed fensucker. Alloyal
subject of the cryptofact, laceface
of the masterace's verseform is sighrhyme
or shims a flashowy weaklink.
I could feel her eyes scrape against me,
the defleshed spirit of kingfisher
naming herself in water
somewhere I have never been flows into me
like the speech of people I have not seen
poetrayed in one noseconed second
in risk-capital's panglossary
tirralyrical senseinsurrection
goldages the dandly crystallion
aerial dead stream through the hair
in the form of radio, conversations
that the trees elbow apart. My own mind
I throw it in the air and as it
falls, it glitters its wings.

Dung Fly

When the pupa unzips its fly the fly
lights out its longing legs and in three days
is laying eggs. Think that rain falls for no
reason. In heaven our shit starts to smell
different until at lunchtime we decompose
in shallow beds and cough down rain
then make wing to ducal paleace
to sculpt open the fecund second.
Flung during its fledge the underhoof
is indentured to our mudhinge.
Give yourself a pat on the back. Thus
the clayey wing-commander slurred
as the slumpthing thicketh its skyeyed
goldrust and fleshes glisten with anusol.
Ears have walls, consciousness
inheres in its matter, then they took away
over those hills. Commerce's mire shall
foster the delicate leaf. The ancient is
more than the sum of the dead, it is the left
sound of a word, it is what successively,
to get this far, they have ruined for us.

Horsefly

I knew him hard. His groundmass of belly,
tined clubmouth that lathed the crypted
fascias, his licherous eyelease
airtasting with tonguepiece for extract of hand
sflesh to follow upwind such sipquid as
humantang. Longsome the trumpetal samethysts
blared and the crystalknight cried:
Harm started me, tinglingered the voltrage,
airboned my goldense instrumentation-boom.
With wingswinging gunturrets
he mouthwatered this warchant then
pricked a puissant stagantler.
Highbeaming his fleshback chemicalsuit
he flew with headrocket to overthrow
the countryside: time wounds
all heels and hounds all wheels. His trumpet
woredown to one song and clouds spilt silence
as a visionmachine with sporadic hair
made sky for a moment hold the lever
of capital. Against this, the ironic
thistles foundered. Songfold the dimstant
metalphor glaxosmithed when the pitot-
booms tonguespiraled. That gadfly which God gave
the state felt streetlight, floaty, like a child
beside a playground in an unfamiliar town,
on holiday, hesitating before joining a game.
We swam in heron-priested streams
and after ran and picnicked. He homed on our
flanks, lay his harms on us
until the welt on the skin loomed too hurt
to lever arm back in to T-shirt. I shivered at
the riverbank. I the horse, he the fly.

Greenfly

I am the weight of a soul,
the flowers stiffen as I
committee the growthroughs
that assetstrip statistic centripetals
visavisages of fuzz and
motets in god's eye, brittle
transcript of air on a leaf
contradiction between leafvein
as air's imprecision gathers.
I leave this in my hands for
your safekeeping, a book on which
is written the insolvencies of cloud.
It takes in airmada of clatteract
and intangelement of deadspirit,
the seethrough scrapemetal, a laser-
etched vasculum, the tulippy
zigzagurat, self as wing, set in shone.
The rain thinks a jettisong
of discontinent mindwindow
dreamforths in a filigreed glasshour
in fadylike selffastening
florifices of tonguerime
& godworn light when my future selves
dismember this entwinery.
Weakwilly the trembular bellstem
awls its illegged misuscle.
A poem must rust or sap the intelligence.
Pale farmers rake clouds. God
got drunk in the seed
and pissed in the flower.

House Flies

I.
Beholed the windowsilly crybynights
stick by their feet to the ceilings: how they
yicker from lightbulbs, tizz in wingwhirr's
tweeters or deathrattle the divisive
panes. Their rotored feet with lunchencrusted
lustre land on the lightstring. Let them kazoo
unriddles for us to settle, knowing
fame is visited on things I just touched
—laptop, coffee-cup—by soul-animals,
heatseeking and watchful. The smutches
they give burn surfaces away to show
the real lives we cannot leave since poetry
is the wrong or no mirror. It is not
they fiddling at the camp gates, not playing
to console: to drown screams, to unction.
Art is palace built on skull-hill, in which we
are the flies' guests, decomposing odes as they
spit night back into its hole, revomit
on sunctioned timepastures, footsniff the
shrill point of the turn. Hold to them, their
legs handwringing in glotten-english
resistance is frutile, exists from retail.
Take those long honey-coloured scrolls
I hung in the outhouse: a month or
a year later I need a bottle of paint-thinner
and open the breeze-block-bricked hole
to a bare lightbulb & there they are, black
heralds, sealed with a wingthin chance of release,
before we will be torches in the fast world,
and dust and dark between us interbreed.

II.

Behind the gilt-grilled lift they hurtlessly
buzz and kneel. When the door slides they follow.
The helmeted airmen's faces resemble
the future. They gaze down nor up. Nor set
nor rise, sensorimotoring in gravity-
negative geotaxis. Their sponge-mouths
feed on airborne soup-globes. Sniff out
the fecal containment units. Footnoting
the lightclots they idle the trip, fiddle-legged.
Through cracked-glass roundels a shimmer
of wing-gauze. Magnetotails of the oftengolded
sun are metadetails. The masses are
staining the plains. Name the city, its legs.
Earth's snowcaps are mould on an orange. Only
the restless will surges among the stars.
So many grains of sugar, so much lunch.
Under the sun's midden anger this eager
rubbing will be love: empty the world into
the eye from which the dead pour down to make
it work with a zero returnrate.
The module is iridescent, hard-eyed. Its
stubby legs will lay them on the moon's wound.
Bound to the soundless void, Neil and Buzz.
Canopen it and they rush intoward
the far-fetched starlight, eggladen, glad.

Unnamed Fly

So many flies you can't see what the
object is. His mother wipes them
away and for a second, you see
the child's eyes open, and understand
this is the news.
In the moment his mother
gestures them away, you see
the seconds left, their swarm,
the child who will be blown soon
to a world in which there is no film.
In front of your dinner the sound
is turned down, because upstairs
your children are sleeping.

Hoverfly

An elemeltary cryptengine trembules
in rappleture, sifting sunlight,
descensory, geostationary, throwinging
the howeaver thether hoverovering
wherover the floweather offers
a nerverse peroration windhoovering
to airsupport the abacusbeadhead
as if their lives depended
birds can't catch the rhythm
the motionblur is in uprose.
As clouds climb down ropes of water
to hustle shadows under the appletree
a scrupulous clubtongue
is nerverending the mindsounds
in vespiform prevocative as
images leak from air as on a broken
laptopscreen a crack breathes sky
through many kinds of light
the sun crashes in flames
touchwhich the errorplane
of interporetation, its accessorized
undercarriage, its farawry eyefilm
overflies the hovels, the hotels.
To heal the sunset tilt the earth.

Lacewing

The light is barely sufficient to bear me.
Blackberries suckle on sun, a thistle
clanks. A leaf is nervous, consider
my damascened cosmostume. Material ghost
I sing whirlwhen the heatwavers
your order was fulfrilled by unchangels
who sew artisan sequints
and telemarket mindescapes where
dockleaves cleave raincarnations
newsprint samethings in leaflike indivision,
selfassembling inveintories of rosetainted
stainedglasses. Head for the trees' sybillines,
their hedgeselfs gladden in song they
built themselves pipedreamily from smoke's
seepages, as if light and sound are
one. The aetherplane caesures the glasblast
I am wrapped in the message the skyhead
carries home it will strut to the self's outside,
unrestive inspectre that avatars braingrains
that a foot sinks as the floor hovers out of vision
but when you turn your eyes I move as
well as air permeates the leaf become
apart in their roads as night's mass unhinges
their senses, forces the ghost from the skin.
In delyrical delicatation I billow from
the table or steel the eyes in the head,
rotate the clocks to see the tangle that time
built. Overleaf, the same poem reinterprets.

Midges

I.

The assembly wheeled like an ill ghost
like brevity's soul, shadow's articulator
howavering in V-winged avionics
with noseconed onescapes zithering.
Like a field of gray-coated mechanics it
mistwisted the slyverse in spontaneous
generations thin enough to be made of cloud
and acknowledge a pain that insisted them
into these shapes: sputnick, public, smut.

II.

Ruddy Phebus gan to welk in west when
it spoke of a scarcely credible love
it said powered it over the fields and
in dance interpreted sunlight scything
oakglades. In this spondeed twing and frong
a fork of light wordwindled into the face
of white. Gyrocoptors immaterialized
as atomsonata or wailful choir
in sunlight's corporation made air aware.
Its words congressed in a dark mine
where nights deposited their leavening dusts
in hatched water that the dead unnumbered
day murmuring small trompets in the twilist
the moon crusting. Sperm was the angel of
dampness. The words required the poem to ask
will we repair heaven in time: break
it into so many pieces, it is still unstill.
Patch it up again with salt and paper.

III.

On the crowded concourse in late November
we flew among you, unannounceable
of cloak, leaving you asking is this state,
large in mind and full to overtop, for
which let art be name of power, second to
sun as the gyre is each day wider
our smoke-formed demiurge heaves a sigh,
each galaxy an ejaculate diffused
not connected with matter until by orbital
association the sides of the push are
exhausted, yields will, and attracts mass to
itself—and then comes the consequent stone
such as the cloud that you hold as 'arm, hand'.
Passing the fossil hospital the gravel
contorts, the trees clothed in teethed birds.
Among us we chose a king but dare
not flee, our operation has no certainty
some soak the florets some gather kisses
on cloud-edge our inner machines work on
explanations that begin on the lips
as the rain ungums the moon. Open
the sweven the steam at the end of the shout
where we are going is into song
the milk stars at miniature hour open
in our world, you wake to find light mix
against a determined sky and come out
fearing. Many hold their heads strangely in
an enmeshing of senses: light snows in
a mirovian causation-cascade
of krill as its seasides rise. Will's
last triumph will be next year's ecstacy.

Mosquito

I.

She is a god of sheer,
arrives in any town
a few minutes after you forget its name;
the desert stretches inside
her grain-of-sand cockpit.

She manifests as a drilling-rig
flown in in secret, preassembled
down to the last
as Rockadrill in treetop.

Nasa accidentally coded hunger
and gave her no neck so
she can't look back.

Test-drilling until
the results are positive,
all she needs is one drop

until there are no swamps left to drain.

II.

Lighting on the side of Zenophila's ear
whisper into it this: I lie awake expecting you.
The evening has stretched far, it has been
a fine day but now the skin mounds behind us.
In every flesh is mistake so Rockadrill corrects
all axes: pitch, roll, and yaw—triggering
spikes like arrows in a movie about
an empire losing as I
crouch in collarbone hollows with great

tediousness and pain sucking haem
aquiver with mineral love, in Zenophila's
other ear find no stalk nor motor-dream will let me
enter. If there were fewer lives time would be
slower, striplights blink. Dancing us to offices,
polyphony of the phoney. What
have we to hold against the authorial
manager, who can imagine this away,
our name. Attach the poem to the list, un
disclose the recipients: information in
the wrong order, sorepoint of the turning world.

III.

The sun sets half a meter away,
the moon is absent. Puddle
is where sky backups clouds.
Evensung in pontine fastnesses
she deepseeps from fensucked
faerials, gunruns a helicopterror
deep into territory, sensefolds.
Her mostquoted nobodiment
thrustabs the thinskins of departing
daylights. A screaky assassinsong
affixes to the starmament
to coillustrate a speculative ullabye,
run herself to air. Autumn violinventions
have minds of form to curflew
on your woundtrack until the screak
is listlost. Dustward her ringarosary
wingwiring mobilizes the untelligentsia
almost surceasefully.
Daybroken clouds stunt the sun. The trees
grit their roots. Where the light inches,
hear the suck of a lifted hoof.
The TV breaks the news slowly.

Stonefly

Under range of dim roomlight to partial shade
was no insertion of aedeagus into capsule
but spontaneous eversion followed by sperm-
convey to external pocket and subsequent
sperm-aspiration by telescoping of female
abdominal segments after tactile stimulation.
Genes nanchung and inactive vibrated
the third antennal segment. Male S-shaped
its abdomen around side, gaining juxtaposition
of terminalia with subgenital plate
engaged female plate with lobes of 10th
tergum pulling it away from genital
opening, initiated packing-action using
epiproct to form cuplike depression.
During this step the up-and-down side-to-
side motions of abdomen resembled actual
copulation: pulsations occurred at 0.5-2s
intervals. With each pulse was touching
by male subanal lobes on ninth sternum.
Midway a bulge was evident at genital opening
indicating turgidity and tubular membranous
aedeagus spontaneously everted,
curved between cerci and mucoid sperm-mass.
Aedeagus was then retracted and male engaged in
brushing or tapping on female cerci.
Female began rhythmic retractions
of abdominal segments behind genital
opening, aspirating sperm-mass. Male
abdomen curved down to side of female
abdomen, then pulse of after-longing.

Scorpion

Once under a time and beneath the moon
the eye on grey terrain tracks other eyes
the meatwands and feelery digits by
which search-data sight, question flame. Think
like stone; sink like sand, wound the heel, issue
a tree the leaf of which curdles things
through head-openings on the trailed moon
that crawled into senses long behind us.
We mirrordrown our vectims with machine-
breath, headstrike the stonehinge, cut the middle-
man for love is our endonym with which
we instring the illominate unstrument
by rule of claw and law of cruel, by
stone will answer stone, spilling units of
harm. Revenge is a chilldish: the strings
run cool. The act of reading brings alive
the indoll with prick and tong the oracle
for sand derives us from tact and the stars
are caught out too long by our answers.
We forest the shadows, are nothing but that
which our name is full of: take head, surge
from rock, seize power while the people raise
cactus-flowers: our children might sing in
the world trade abstracted. A failed state's
ruler starts from the wasteland. Tails, he wins.

Pseudoscorpion

Secondly, when one eyelash of yours falls past
midnight my shadows rush to take it,
Over the grey peneplain nothing moves
apart from god's hand and then some stillness
hurtles from me—I, beetle-driver, custodian
of dust, beleague the loopholes and the labourynth.
In order to polish language's mirror
and climb the last sentence I forklift
pedipalp, foremitten and eyesuckle
all alliable in a junkbonded counter
memory unevening the crepuscule, my clauses
depend from the wreck of a fly, hingeable
jawpiece. The stones are thinking too hard.
Hold till you see the whites of their eggs.
The dark is under attack from more dark:
the father and the man in robes let me do this
in my meetings with the stone floor.
My hardgot rockdrill fragmented. Affix
spit light, maps come out in the head
to express how our forested smallarms are
as we had laid our brows, the bowls
combine elegy with the toes in the sand
the sun, old fried, its trail turns black
to the golden empires of the child.
In death's innumerable rubble it sees
the snake lay in the sun then it crepes up
at the tail & so to the head but then
he claws him softly & he fastens so
hard that the snake cannot shake him of &
this beest sleeth him & then eats his full.

Tic

Tics, commuters from the dead
clenched woodpiles of sense
extraneous as time is to the objects
on which they hang, resting
stimulessly in skincases with
no ideath but inthings. Stars prickled
with contempt, senses congregated on
the path submitting to night
when the velcrobat climblimbed the stalk
event-managing the fieldedge
under the velluminous evenstar
towards umwelt's metastable sepulcer.
Its 12-year moment beclipsed until
one butyric senseme and it skydived
to foothook a mammalian hahair.
Once on the embodily matterhorn
of a trunk it fulltilted its gramatom
pinhead, jammed its joycetick in the slurface
and bloodlet a cuplet of globs to
oillwell its invisceral earnout.
Plumplump the doughdoughty roly-
polyp, queen of gloat, aslaked
oblivious bleeding as a corrective
to the bleedingly obvious.
Bladdered & quasilazy it eggdropped
embodily and teetered tickstock.
By the otherity infeasted in me (it spoke)
grotund dustrust of the foreheadow
I fuelfilled the clandestiny nonthing
for fullupped on bloodmeal, I
reassisted language almost surceasefully.

Silkworm

In my sleep, I see the poem I am working on, its layout:
shorter lines than normal, an abstract, difficult page.
I look at the words, knowing that when I wake
I'll forget all of them and have only the image.

She was not filial, and she treated her in-laws
badly, so the Silkworm Mother punished her.
Not far away stood a white-dressed lady.
Between ether and sense her wound yielded
milk-of-bone the which in her womb changed into
wool in manner like a spindle. She was waving:
Ah-Qiao looked up, in front of her appeared
a houserow with white walls and shingles.
The trees' glossy leaves were larger than
her palms. Many white-clad ladies carried baskets.
"Little girl, what a rare guest! Come play with us!"
In the day she picked leaves and at nights
fed them to the white caterpillars, until that
which was before a creping worm had now wings.

The dream continued, we can contain your work.
It will be made of page, crudely drawn, leaning into
the sunset as exile as snow where men felt them
selves open. I replay the revisions of river into an ever
unchanging line of production.

They spun walnut-like snow cocoons.
The ladies taught Ah-Qiao to pull
and color the silk threads that were to be worn by
the heaven-gods. One dawn she left, without
a goodbye, took the silkroads with her
sheet of fresh-laid heavenworm eggs.

Woodworm

I made a false star. It was flesh to dry.
Few spoke of this, but the heroes leaving
the song composed monographs on time
in which animals were quotations
looking forwards out of their pens or
boxes, mahoganic auras of glutenberg
indentured for snailyears inside the lumber:
how do you tell your dreams or play
the tempered clavier upon the tree of
clocks. I deathwatched the wormwould.
Machinebrides emptied the hole where
the suptimbers ambered and in resinsong
longing's atrophy was morsed by chisel
of deskbound child-labourer. Speech
issued from them. The poop they sat in was
floorbored, intangled in nightash where
ingestments did great scathe. Shepherds danced
eclogues, clogged dances, piped pastorals
the devil of the wardrobe abraded
among sweepings and leavings. Tabernacled
in rust were inbuilt lockclicks nightwounding
like a cogito downprinting unearths.
Outbeings of gold, I turned my anger into art
my eyes to cages, but the watch against
time was lost, stillburnt language was
our issue and tissue, child and binding.
Ash opened where face broke off
boled with a lullabrade meltality
that eked the rockadrilled antiques.
A healed field is an end to rivers, read
them down to oak, embodiment's
image in wood. They saw me for dust.

Thrips

Fastfwd the scaleself
that atomsplits the rootworld
and tropes the fleshlight
in statistic siftiness in profile of
gridded submarine
in the game of Battleship, pipthrips
kilned into desire with what
you mishit. The splinters of
humed summer when we cleared nettles
certainted an inertitude
until upon us landed these signs.
Each scale has its *punctum indifferens*.
One is cartesian apostrophe.
The headhole isitself atissue as it
pezdispenses implemelts in their palaces.
The therivative rootfoot is in
jewel-cases & gilt picture-frames.
There is a self at the end of the
finger in the slept dust:
inseity of its fluked being.
The animals destroy nature by
deploying thought-fragments
that emdash through aether
a cogitatory iamb adheres to clothing
to seethe the claggard minutiae.
Semicolonize your skin in finitessimal
embodimelts. Crisistalks continue in
to dwindliness. Language divides its
elf in a poem the dust lifts to reveal be
tween a leaf these smithers sinking
an underdome descreed. Sing how the house
fell off me while I was asleep, I slept years
in the liftable paperflap
heart in Descarte's *De Homine*.

Cockroach

All around <blackbox> stand the cones of men
shuffling as the wind, with no west for the ricked in
whomever tricklocks the wainscot
say the indurate seekerhead its
eledgy, nightfails the feelery as a stored
potato eyes the humean crackery with
scuttlery tremblimbs. Find behindoven
the liquefact. <Blackbox>'s mechanized
shoes burn away in daylight, it means
shit to squinch with a piston's insistence
and lofty brow of the philosopher
to sup on stuck ghee, feather the margarine like
oval soul-animals, to chemtrail the
insensong malalignments as begun-
again clacketting towards the longunsung cache
from which with breadcrumbs and a pipette
they coax wings from <blackbox>'s carevice
and musculo-skeltonic cloacaraca.
Wormwards the nightworn devil's cow
drives <blackbox>'s bloodhissing coach. Each hour
empties itself on <blackbox>, fukushimal
animist, the government at the end of fingers
engrosses the encroached scenetrail from such
stone. <Blackbox> grows rootlegs
and swingarms out of the picture. We are like it
in those respects that it is alien to us.

Dung Beetle

When at eve the beetle behemoth
and the rain clots in the car's genitals
our language turns to the road, the light as if
inside we drive uphevil with God as windshield
between us and the rest. These thoughts are
not words, but have the quality of being
understood. Irreconcile with shard-
beetle as it genghisses its heavesong. Oblique
motions, light-edged corners strum.
At Uluburun call him Aksak, elsewhere
Square urine-squirter, big rock beaver, hump
backed flute player, earth-mover, cowturd bob.
Senses gather him against the dung. Flollop
the crowbarred scarabapple through
ozymandates, scrunch the matterhorn pelt
a merdchant for the duchy. Observe
the disapparition of these faeces in a cloud.
Sun leaks from a wound that must but
cannot be located. When cattle package
leaved grass behind them he uprears, waves
his sensorium and Sisyphus-
footed knocknees his fussball, exits
the hard-hat area to plantcross with load
bearing carapacity: follows the galactic
whey-marks across the urnfield to dungfork
our spilth, stand guard while the female digs
broodchambers. A far-future adrifts from
the system and when we lift the urns
from their earths in free space we look
for a new star before the moon rinds out.

Glowworm

No sentence is complete
in a pale park the ghosts of slain warriors
discharge into the vast
they dim, they seem this unminuted midnight
to alluminate the moonsyllable
with a lampyrid paralullaby
twastold that the twinedlight jackalants
spectred norwhere in glimorous
foreverie, to heatseek the indivisual time-
consumer as a dimmer-switch
mists the waxend at undown
with policelights electrickling.
This map of the world at night illustrates how
the phosphored flightbulb
unextinguishes utility's lightclot
a gluttering navlight neverywhere
that Mary went a plasmascreen
or spectrail twilist is a sign-
machine sloshing sunup
stars until we are the information we need
the imprecision at the end of the limbs.
Fading behind that cloud
strange music invertebrates
the cones of men as the wind gems in circles
in that time the stars careless in their love
accumulated in the head a deeper
sleep. Comets never forth but when
is great rain this worm quenches the fire
like a plate of ice and if a man's body
be touched with the dung of this worm
all the hair of his body shall fall.

Ladybird

I.

I structure this poem like a story so you may
understand there is no story.
All is frame, tomorrow never less
when thoughtswings above like
the breath of knowledge,
the sun still burning its banknote
the hindwings under their cases visible
simmering milk under the lid
the cow of the lord will
measure me for my wedding glove.
A period of weeping intervenes
until she drains from her mask,
rejoins the carriageway of your palm
unsettles on the skin, stands ajar.
Art is dead between us, my thumb
understands. Polish it so we
can see our real shapes where we dream
oftly and on the undertimed fragments
her face is a lineage, it wounds by looking:
people cascade in her shadow, its
flowers speak their minds
on the fungal flesh of garden furnishings
in the world that is the case waves
and attitude wait under tunnels
remember as a child remembering as a child
the boot-shiny pedalcar
the rust fixed where the helmet loosened
were words missed on this
and the silence of the children is harder than
the noise they used to make.
The songs do not think they will stay long.
Roses arreared, roses she blew,
she drove her bloodred slaveships over to you.

II.

Receipt of a magical agent. This is at first not known as such. The members of a family are enumerated, and the future hero is giftwrapped in notional costume, Barnaby goes counterclock, his feet disarmour our wingmirrors, slow words transmit dollars and furies, and we inch into an age without reception.

Unrecognized arrival. Moon's sister is introduced and her status is indicated on the occasion of her first menses. Wingcase-bonnetted Barnaby dabs. Queen mab and king mob arrive, one by limo the other on foot, there is a spatial translocation between kingdoms.

Unfounded claims. The hero of the main tale is the heroine's as yet unborn son, demigod child of the king's unmarried sister by her brother. Barnaby dreams of a noddy car again, among the irises, siding through thick woods towards Glenthorne. The children are waving as I grow smaller over the hills, the balloon of me. My other car is a metaphor, my name is unwit. He smells the presence of a human in the spittle.

Difficult task. He must carry water in a sieve, reeve a thread through a log, make a rope out of ashes, a drum that sounds without beating, sort ash from lentils, cut water. Make a shirt without cut or seam or thread, washed in a well where water never was and dried on a hawthorn that never sprang, till an acre with a thorn, sow it with ice, harrow it with a thread, tack it in the sea, and fetch it home dry. The seeker decides upon counteraction, and the interdiction is violated. Barnaby wends his wings towards the windflower's dreamword. Mother-breath flickers among the flat roses as by sign of storm he succumbs to none in holding the river down, singing time helps me die where thrushes gather at page corners to behold the stormed leaf, the opening word. Defunct star with lyrical eye: unsick seamistress, Barnaby.

Solution. Barnaby changes from human into the sun so he can tie a thread to an ant, put a maybug inside a drum, add weevils to the lentils. Grow a new suit. Seven is the quality-ascent number here. Dweller-in-state among the dreamwitted he hemispheres the metamessage.

Recognition. Under the sign of face the mask of Barnaby: to know you for the first time he dryhumps the rosebleed until our truculent volkswagens are carwashed. Butterfly unanswers, showing willingness to assume the role of hero.

Exposure. Heroine and Villain join in direct combat. Muttercar is a mastercar, Barnaby jiggery-pokes the rosicrucian she-mother who is unowner of the western vernacule. A tiger tells his mother to prepare the unborn fetus for eating. Moon's sister lacks information concerning the whereabouts of her mother who is redrendered among the faunature.

Transfiguration. The face surfaces, in midflower the jowly spadix lolls its gross perfumes. Out of the Foxglove's door toll forth my death, then to my burial come. Barnaby bugwing is daylighted, spit-and-polishes his thumprint. The storks flying overhead attract the attention of Moon's sister, and she has a presentiment that metaphor is what we travel in.

Punishment. Most indefatigably is the birch applied to Barnaby. The heroine is liquidated by the riverbank as waves untie the sand's unities to the ends of the spoken world. Barnaby has to make payments to see the children. Moon's sister greets and interrogates the donor, bumblebee, who twice stings the heroine to death. In a negative sense she has found a home.

Wedding. Our glowing reports state Barnaby weds with two michelin star eyes and one season waiting behind the other like trains, each driver in appropriate regalia: the waggon-spokes made of spinners' legs, the waggoner a grey-coated gnat, will seize your eyes. Make the world dance Barnaby.

Whirligig Beetle

We had been watching clouds
make copies of themselves,
a jet-trail like a flaw in an empty glass.
In his small craft sat Lewis, vortician
of the evereverberating rowback. He
shivered his uppermoist pondmotor
torrented those quasilly facetiae
while glossuaries of gigularity
palpitated the aeioulian metallurge
in circumcentric cascades: agoggle
in slapstic spastic wrongoing.
The instantaneous then of the image
clocklocked the clauseway with
our angels, their structures
facefacetted with bifocal touchscreens
fictioning inbeside a leetlet's
irreverberate waterial, the star
and-start-architecture combined
without pause, metallic fascia
on the pond that is made of eye
rowlocking rushstrokes to a
wheely scribbled throbstance,
paraddling indurabble dabbles while
the shade concerning my skin also
moved behind me, and it felt
waterthing is wavewoven wordfold
as, slowly, in the fulness of space
the words destroyed themselves.

Museum Beetle

I ate a crocodile in its enormous suit
by which I stored some rich fats that in
the winter months hatched inside you, visitor.
I reactivated fossils. My ingestigations
took years, leaseheld the hauntiquarian
cabinest my plastron gorged on clattercombs
when I chewed through the furline manuscrape
and cockchafed the semilunar vellum
deseeded Japaneseries and dimslit arkworks.
Under the head metals melted the hand
felled the noses from the monuments
that stringheld an indistinctive sunlight
channeled as a gemgleam in the sunbeam
attracted to myself by motion—and
then the solvent in time's ripeness, when I
irreplaced the jarred airs clogfooted
and knuckledusted the awkworld clockery,
consumed wunderkammersful of vellum
alphabeasts the babelbodied pelts of
archivalries rearchived and daubed
in flamethyst's featherdust hooverbagloads
of mothember, hornate treasuries
I lunched upon plastic unrealisations
then revandalised the hidebound display-
cases nihilating such illexible tapestries then
ate my way through language found the forms
loaded in the eye, supped clock and gut
and fluff, perished thoughts to disenchant
self, that engine of workings and horn.

May Bug

The metallurgent submissile windowstrikes,
flipsides, cockchafes. Boeings into the gap.
Gription torques the droning flightwheels, to do
in the head, to fight back through the slots.
Whose diary consists of torn autumnal leaves telling
headventures of the furzeowl that flocks
his archambers. I tell the child apart
when balaclaved shadowmalcules in
rentacar getaways use earchaisms
such as brackenclock is carbonnet
so we heave the gongbeaten soundvalues
of menchanical bombards to be
protomouse, motoreyed metalmorph
taxiing on the tabletop to inch
senseitself. Turretted midself
unchanges its sectary. Dumbstrikes its
wingribs unevening the oakweb's misfits.
I break my body open to see if
inside my wingcases the days move and
sound comes apart on inspection:
I robot, ply on ply with the beaten
wings of the longdead that the second wipes
away. Humbuzz of kommerz. Wings schwitter
to the floor. Stars weep energy. A key
in the frame the door swang. We reopen
the enquiry when the stains have been removed.
Loops and twists follow. When is adornot
a dor? when a thread of violence suspends
that force circumstance dreams of, a story
branching on the table and government where
the sheds should be. I think I ruined your life.

Sexton Beetle

Work hurt us open. We used the dead for
our own ends and on their time but the window
called with great clarity, it amassed the light
under the trees when the wind skulked
beside its wall, fleshholed the claymold as from
the cellar a figure gestured upwards scattering
pinches of prayer-meal with admixture of
finely ground sea-shells, saying:
in each village is a drain into which
the dead shall pour, a symmetry where
hewn smells correct the mosthighest flowers.
When a mammal dies it releases huff, we sift
air with our headfans to bioassay
the slowworn sussurections, ambulance-
race the dead. When I closed my eyes, I heard
my father voice a thin earth between us,
helicoptering down as Doré's Satan in
an airhearse while light emptied in tendresses
we brushstruck the soilid ratbones
hamsliced mouseskulls, shrewpelt, molebone
a few frigid reluctant stars worth
mentioning only because of the light
they expended on us, pittance of being
the other people who surrounded us
dimglimmered through sleeps written in
Hare's peerage, a long underground book
probeable in the sweatshop of the buried.
What we can speak about together is clogged,
poetry travels under fine soils, raising
head nor talus between work's engagements
and the conclusion that the egg is.

Stag Beetle

I.

No entry without id.
As pincher-machines enforce night
the wood inbreathes, smeone
bleeds smething: nose-horn, scuttella,
pectinicorn scarabaeid.
When the skeletons drive from the leaves
they park close to each other
and jumpstart without leads
the boniferous car. The pinchbug
wife probenoses deliberative
to the implements. Offers
eyelash tinting and laser hair removal.
Wait, I shall assemble you some flowers
and a complaint against the sky.
The husband runs a semi-legal wheel-
clamp operation: achieves a high roll
over rate despite being analphabête
and watches a cloud come to mind
fearfeels his deerantlered head-case
in a synisthesis of unction
towards some dreadful equipment
purring in the grass. It is innermoist
mindnight in the hartshorn nothinge:
speechacts its anatonym,
runalongs a chatteract.
We see him microcamerangled.
Our frequencies say he
would be car-boned, crumplezoned.
Truculent skin works loose, foldaroll
we fall over, fallala,
the ancient days surround us.

II.

Activate the dust,
snouted gods of the innerworld.
Plentiful in form like makes of phone,

under snap-open hoods there are
pistons elbowing letter-by-jawpiece,
deriving song from sap.

One of them goes to the stereo and starts
the almost unworkable engine
of a Beethoven quartet. They prefer
stringed music,

headed by disciplines of smell
their jawed helmets clusters
at holedamp, understone, leafshield.

Their mouthpieces speak of
tippling on our floor,
are heard in scrape language,

glossed in early evening pieces.
Their Arthurian lances twitch from
a fallen log's portcullis.
Oil sumps from their armours.

They go to seek the night inside the plum,
imprint of the apple's decay,
bugled pales of lost chivalries.

Japanese Beetle

From the cemetery bench I face the dog
rose, eat salad, notice a flowerhead
move in no wind, see a green beetle
cropping the stamens. From
the mouth of it floats an oblong soap-
bubble, desideratum of war.
The only earth he held when he went
down is what is caught between his nails.
Earthgrains pant like heavy plant
crossing, silver-greaved, pale one of Epirus
casts spears against himself, in female seed
reaches out, hooks a crumb in mixtecan
belief that their heads round in the soil
godhead turning towards the future stars
irenically mudhooded with pollens
and warsbreadth of scarabic swordplay.
He shritches and glades. Leafflitters
his fairings in the moonslit woodland. To
dwell in bone-built homes, in rodent-head
or regalia of tree, refractive shine of umwelt
rotates a galapagan solarpanel,
carcaresses a verbrich eithereality
to selfserve the verduring undernearth
the scrolling leaves that unsettle
as he beats in the void his shelly wings
in vain, holding in his teeth the charcoal left
from the bone fire. Englandanger
the hardhatted rebels who push through
bramble, post up h and s edicts
concerning the fact these stones may fall.

The Spider

I.

In the headlights' trickery
a leaf lies bleeding.
The hangman scaffolds the truncated tree.

A frailty, a possibility, thin as the moon
in the hallway. There's a spike in
thinking, an early breeze.
A rootless plant makes
sense of the edge you slice through
the door. The nylon
draws tight. Sequined and sequential
each eyelet calculates chance.

It spent the night supping husk of fly
and poises on the second
it can split. It tenses.

Each page of its book is black.
That scaffold it built: soon
I'll be light enough to climb it.

II.

You are curled in death like you were too cold
an image of you sleeps in the mouse
is tangled in beds: pulseless seamstress
for whom the trees make sense

over a pallet a grab suspended
the air was taken from

there are birds left in which liquid spoke
and seconds to none. Each motion
ends with the finger
dusted in answer

you tell me shadow is sex of the moon
ask me in how many languages
does the shadow drip

spider of us, I cannot say.

III.

As voltaic leaf-engines start their motors
it fills it darklung belly with chainfood
jumps böng böng and has kidneys nor
heart. Staminal sap moves upon the span-high
eyegrab, reinking the spinsense to shem
where exculpated exilarch shall retread.
When you seize its beard, it counts years
by shrieks and gales, spends itself upon
the marsh, emits ropes and clothing with
feedfork. Totethered at anglement's end,
swayed by early waking, so gatefolded
deathshed's dimsister. Anansi among
the Anasazi, a Nancy among reichs
tautens the tongueply that spinenters
the startle-reflex of staved unstruments
as it crouches before the news. Heavy-
bubbed substance, lull the limbs,
rent iron from scrapeyard orchard
pad down that spiral stair partake of name
the bowmen of Shu in racing attitudes
are full of seemings, the mucharmed bowmen
of Mons draw back their barbed and telegraph
wires. The past teeters, the state steadies,

rocks. Shadow's giacometry ruinsides us.
A spider scrawls out of Europe,
fistfirst, handfast. Jack is out of the box.

IV.

With its overarm it lifts the sheet of dawn, flashes in the development
display. With its nuclear arm it hosts thread-built threats, antifreezes
miscast strictures to tether threadbreadth's tristress and ensnarl the
attenuated loom. With its investment arm it lattices the browser
with orbed dew, releases the catastrophe-bonds, initiates austerity's
stringencies. With its youth arm it roses the threadimensional stars:
their scope is horror. With its smallarm it draws the wire to dance
in sissyfoot of disarray, applies surgical dressing. With its harmarm it
shackleashes the widerangling cast, prefabricates fingered applications
in Braqueish discreation of traffics. With its swingarm it tunnels the
remembody of streaming sun, weaver of rainbursts. With its grabarm
it disentwines from crawler of mossquiet searches, maximises the
portential, navigates pages, manages vibratory traffic, breaks in to the
universe to steal its dead and populate our stars. With its air arm it
trawls for equity. Quickly catches krill in the net. Waves clickbait into
a pursenet. It can't see who was estranged, suspects world is wide and
worse than any seatangle. With its secular arm it agitates semantic links,
surf. Spitsticks prey, angles its stabilimentum, reassembles the night-
broken lines. Few are the figurers-out of it funnels; most fail.

V.

This time we precede the ruin.
The water walks towards us
as if it has something to say.
The trees are armed with

birds, polyglot and atonal.
Across acres and meanders

geese perfect their laughter.
Tall willows point into the mist

and the grass hunches under it.
The weir tells as ever how
patches of light become stranger
to each other. Everything had seemed

precise: the silk-fingered signposts,
a clogged fly. Then
like absence in a Chinese scroll
the mist repeals, the light

is sweeping. Horses crop, no longer
where we put them. A thumb-smudge of
tree at the bottom of a page, no more
than real. A heron walks

professorially, and the light, as water,
bequeaths from the trees.
The spider is dressed so tightly
it does not have room to reflect.

Blood Spider

If instead of language we had
a universal map so that each thing aligned
uniquely no two objects
could have the same identity, and
all numbers would then sing
agency in every crack of being,
clogging fleas' feet with accuracy
for what could we thread days with
then but this evermoving pucker
that clothes the limbs of self,
and from that wound flaws not
words but the coordinates of being.
Thus theory must account
for consciousness's rust across
a finger's arc, unnoticed
smear on the framing glass.
An end is in itself, the air sweats
at the glass's falling. Then the wind
slept me away to asterisky
approximations of the motelet
packing a lullabide of the phasma
malgazed into indefinity by
tainct of spurt-spirited moloch.
They sing: Turn to sand the clocks, their missions.
Enter the works of the nearest machine.
Entropy is our end, render us then
Marses unwrought from
sky, seeking each night a fix, suff or pre.

Garden Spider

The Duchess of Webster, breakleg listener
to stars, many-fisted archenchantress,
gardener, ashdowager, gatelegend, is
discovered in dumbshow hunged
on the spoked bicycle that connects nights
with the fingers of a cellist. Time was her maiden
name, she clumb the shadow wall
when excess defined style and we came
through chaos singing down
strutmachine she can ropewalk to the nearest shrub
in the fork where mind rotated
into descendless porehistory otherwise
with her kohled eyes she hedged alphabets.
Nobel shake-rags, the helmet shall no longer
harbour her, she ascended to tell
the moon how to feel among the thorn of crowns
a thistle clanked then the substance
fell out of her but she worked upon herself, and
extruded webs admirable for fineness
of thread, but of no profit from her touchpouch
the sky paid out ropes and she fixed things
was law a prison to entangle those that
nightjarred the tenuous space of thread, thereat
to set appetite as theatre. To lean alone
against the moon she dreamed lobed beings
backwards her self in silken sepulchre
distillated an estringed vengeance as
the souls of her came to deadleg craneflies
they feasted their filmsy stickfingers
brokered the limescale lostlaughs.
Slowly the formworld limplimbed in bemusic.
When the worms pierce your winding sheet
make a thin curtain of your epitaphs.

House Spider

When the waste-disposal-apparatus gristles
and inserts spill from the property-section
we travel lightly over wronged matter
as santa's silvered sac shakes
the curtains of childhood from
the half open window, and feltering in his
falx his supper he fistlifts and legangles
a gluewet webverse belimed in threadition
with subspecious reticulum
teetertops a vibratory tropedance
violing the spirallel stickfigurge
dustangled in tension-headache, grisps
the elasticky floss that thereby
engines a fetish-mask for clustomers:
he had xeroxed spinozan ethics
until he ran out of pages so that
moonody's angleg can infist the
web-worker of opus anglicanum
to declench the ondoyant netwinery
like a house-detective phonehacking
filaments of the sadomasterfist
for weight shines its grisaille orb
asunderstand silkstrikes the upside or
people run towards our voices, telling us
to thread this sentence along the cielung
upon instilligence of threatlevel
shadows at the stairsfoot spindle under
the hand of a magician while a plane cracks
and through the wall-eyes of television
it unclenches because in the hallway
a thinkspike connects aspects to shores sliced
through the door after he spent the night poising
on the second he splits, he tenses, his tenuous
looks have facets of words each
page of his book is black, the fissure king

shares a house with a blade of light drinks sleep
without thirst and the encyster creaks on
its legs and leads to all that's dead and bone
scaffolding the moon in the hallway.

Funnelweb

When Orpheus fallalters his many-stringed lyre
the morning sky fills with loose threads, with
spacewalkers reentering the frostburnt
heathsides with lacyrinths of the seemistress
and nobodily desdescendings through godangled
tangletwine onto bleeds of grass. Sad clouts
on the washing-line, a voice is lost:
come in please. Build a bridgethread with spinneret,
enter by l'age d'or, starting-gate, coital toilets
eyefeel a farangular foldoverol
string a sensearchive by fishingline
or five-barbed beard of wisdom
be ushered by bellman to discover
a dunderworld like an arch of creaction,
twelveyed retiarus on limb-stilts his hourglass-
throat sings each treenerve as the cancer said
to the archbishop my nailed arms would
embrace you were it not for wethorn,
so please open up the false-floor, pulsense
the tropewalkers, watch-dense cloglegs
predate the damselfly and the ideal reader.
I fished with nest supping on husk,
running us out from the lanes where Shelley
sat himself observing the eartomb from
which nature poured to sand, but in dream a
sudden wind blew cold through my clothes in
mazy netanglements the venture-backed
abracadaver was linecaught by counter
demons tripwiring tined foot-bristles in
messageloop who clingfilm me underleaf:
I fall for flesh's anomaly. Love's
ember guide in such folds embeds the dead.

Aphid

Under the window of each cell
a selfabsorbing fundatrix
marginalizes a bestiary
in roserendered gangreenery,
depyxting in her manyscript
firedrakes and mandragons.
Senses open along her skin
like small doors as silence
sleepstalks. Soon her heavenblown
childangels bottleneck the petals
as a subrosa sorority
tweeks the sapstaff.
The pane opens in her face.
Sapdrunk on engodiment she
virginbirths bucolic stemborers
and spandanglers of sappy plantstalks.
Vinevitably their world trucks with
the corrupt as the ants siphon the profits.
Packed with nunaggression
the stemmother's huggermug
tonguestucks in a mastersalivatory
milksap of symbolosis, malengendering
no usurprising, nervetheless
she opensources paracitizens
into a swarmament. She is now
so many, resistered, that
she arranges in descending order,
rosebursts the sugarplump semiself
somehere with her subject eye
until the season returns her to her cell.

Hairlouse

There are no two ways:
language proves he is not fit to live,
the horseman who forages
our scarps and tightfistedly crosssells
his eclogue and squattles
in periwigs and wyliecoats.
We notlice his carbonnet crabuncle
nested to nervendings in velcro
ministring. O heraldic scaffolder,
intanglable peripheralien,
stuckist in the manachinery, goose
fleshing smeddums of tongueglue.
Upsideways inhabitatter! sucker
for lovebony limbclimbs
he jawfastens the scalpscape
overdredges bald pates like white scurf,
watertights the dwindleg, tresspisses
despite hairproduct. God matters
in him like a furbidden bloodangel
to disentangage the wireshirt scurface.
Eggfast in his forefork the night
between his fingernails he urings
the scurfy spirtits, hushstrokes
selvered liplets and tristinguishes
imparticles of maninfestation.
He knows headphone's connections
to earbone, crowlin on the droddums
and domed heads of Europe:
the sunking, sumpthing, clog of tongue's
end are stone against him, felt
eventfuel for the mesothorax, who
seethe others as otherseemen
or tother tethers as selfseeing.
Take my thus words into your hands,
ruin them through your hair.

Woodlouse

I.

Lift a stone, they headlong northearth
carbodily locomoting to
the undercarriage crevicices.
Shelltering from twiglight in dugouts
love's armadillaries roll the pianolid
goffering their palps
to scavenge ismantled orlops,
wouldooze the telltaled zoomort
& wordmouth the etceterratic
uncyclopedia of the unstutterable.
In conversations with night the gardens
harden. If you catch a chalk-giant's
shadow by its feet squeaking home,
compress it until the boots are sunk.
Folderoll the eye of the what that
is left. Poetry made me happen we
say or finish the sentence with
an alphabet trembling through
darks. Word progresses as if of
the stuff of are, inset of self,
lightearthed as rootrotted rockababes.
The winter was buried under litter
the letters aged between their scales
or the sunset expounded through hills.
Step back through the brick escapade.
Hear them in a cupboard in the city
discharging. The road shuntraveled
behind them to the end of
nature: the sea's unhands are
many, and reaching. We come to
the sun, and unforget that we know.

II.

In the garden I kept digging up
corpses, some the size
of a fingernail, and I remembered
my child's graveyard made from
lollypop-sticks and sweet-wrappers.

They came at night to drink
the sweat from our underparts
and brush the strength of our fingers
in the daytime behind the skirting
they composed texts in our praise
clustered around the carpet's Sahara

mud is thickening somewhere
as if an odd requirement stood in the language
a word tipping its scales

you find them caving the fallen apple's
inrotted body, faces packed, scattering
as the light named itself on the ground.

Pondskater

From the bridge I see teams of rowers
arcross the delilium, cracks
in the eye wave-weave the nameslake.
In flagellar schememes
of diatomic cross-selling
they waterclot concentricity
unsentensing waverlengths of twisight.
This is my longtomb partnerve agile,
fragile sky is hinge to
the parallel dark, foreverending
camerangel. The river commissions
a new meadow where the last heat
in a star burns (the phantom photon
enlarges on this) as moons
are rowed and sent thithaway
trireming intimotions or slap
dashadows in noded disjointment
their mittens petaling the sandbeds.
Presisting the intelligence is
furtile when clouds are falling in.
In this way our passage through
days conjugates a lifelung
seismiotic in distorts and
waterlilt semisphere. The pond
quake cruxes into inscensible
nameslicks, tinetingles and waterrings,
as in the skylike is awrighted what
is writ on water: your name, where.

Cricket

I.

Crystalike bell-insect of earstrangement,
lord suzumushi, ever-rephrasing singer
of the self-generating text, horse of
the earth, chick of the god of the hearth,
insistent collaborator with deserts,
chicken of the weaver's shuttle, duke
yu-hu-lu, inhumator of kunstwerkers,
spokesperson for the dead: shake
open your wingshells, hoverwhelm and
mistfeel the sembodied splintergroups.
Each word's paradox, the crossed leg in the
syllable—your sentence has the purpose
of resolving these, to catch a thing alive
in a net of sound, but it sometimes
hurts. Now I am sure we have in
the head a folded sonnet and outside is
one star that can be followed if we concentrate
on the sound there is much working in it but
like a ship it is the storms we pass
through, the navigational zeros, archaic
torsions before the waters of the head
where love lodges a sense of loss
and weeps for us to be children.
In the tenth month you enter our beds:
I the undesigned ask poems to
coimplicate language, stir me a leaf
giving foot to the lines with equipped legs
and to unendulate in the obliteral edgeland
where engines whir behind a thought the puppet's
feet are real, as a hipped fragment inside
an engraved person. Your voice scrapes parch
meant, if bones could collect themselves and hang
flesh then strut towards some westwards river, if at

dawn the cloud is only what the eye rolls
away then, lord, we will know of your state.

II.

There on the table, nearly tipping
on the length of its antennae.

I nudge it into my hand and
its African mask doesn't slip.

It stares through me like an acre of grass,
and blinks itself away.

Grasshopper

I.

Shopper of gras, ply the trades while error
bruises its head on glass. Those the mirror
capture live together in vain. None notice
a wall in which is visible in a corner a door to
the previous room, deskeletoned clouds
listing through a window. The devil
is in retail, asking 'Why did you not
gather food in the summer, like us?'
She replies 'we were sweeting music,
folderold.' In uncertain light we come
upon her sectioned eye in electrifield
the prevailing wind farfallen, love's
fuel is fossible but the best books were
unwritten in the dark, by pundit-maudit's
hoperandi. The rain acts in uncertain
light the crepit dust rises as she chirrs to e
scape the torture of next week's inscape
strokes tightwound as leaves breathe.
Unriverun past sleepread of jigger,
numb nudger, not cricket. The customer service
guarantee states the stars are less on
the axle-tree with her wordlong name: 'What a dust
do I raise!' the rain stops distant tractors burst with
in, part of the story: in dream we
look for the seam that tells all, and put aside
daylight so the clipped moon can see over
a hedge faces blossom against us jumpstarts
the stiffends / make it stronger, stranger.

II.

Thistles had been arming themselves
for months, and grass spears

rub against silence. Tithonus,
gate or wicket keeper and spokeman for
the time-hardened, twitches his celloplane.
Denymphs in nerverending nomelody
lay lethergetic elblows on him and farangle
their chromatic stiringquartet. Writing this
I crick my nick and drunk my agatey
metalchine, evensosing the screenshot
shiverses to and froth the wheatwave
wordwards as secretangents crowdsource
his headphoneme and zithery violince
against woofers in facet-time. The
stones in their undreams shape like lies, candles
of self burn against an image which is
poor until probed. The flowers come
apart and light interrupts the sixleaguebooted
furtherer in midstridulation as the cat
rolls on his path and windows open by
themselves. A second flowers. When
the emperor looks through the Moon Gate
the angles weep inside him, machine-senses
work in their moving little languages
& in the stead of mouth a little tongue
licks the dew and thereby he cheerups.
She has been stranged by her husband
or an unknown aslant. Time's enemies sing
as birds in the silent march: with virtuoso eyes
the fields are rape with mancorn margins
where once he lept until in sense the tired earth
broke idea from song. Could he
fit a future that is anything but repetition
as though the ambulances kept arriving
to complicate the lyric and
music's recurring place in this language.

The Locusts

Before the first air was raised or the dark unlet,
the locusts were stirupped for battle
with faces of dim-bodied unsettlers, galoshed
and helmeted, their superstruts bonerung
and their hair as the hair of women, their teeth
like teeth of lions: and on their heads
I placed crowns: who handspanned this world-arch
hewed crowds of them, foddered them on straws,
unstringed their ramshorn syllables, airboned
these fingerwidth timepests that crooked their lipped mouth
partings and visited them upon the dwellers
in the house of being, that the rush of their wings be chariots.
I bid them overrun the great halls,
uncover the temples, bring down the choirs
and strip the fields. I who you buried in
the name of the idea of God wrang
out heaven's clout until beggary over-ran
the Commonwealths, arable was salt, crumbs
of dried flood spotted the meadows, a third
part of the sea became blood, heat sang
in wounds as my finger moved, amused
myself with such fireworks as people,
leveraged drouth from hope, then hope from
drouth, and in some particulars doing this
felt aliver, but still could not say 'I live'. Thus
in come time I graze the timesoiled roads in
my shining cage, the light having been let.

Slug

Roots riot overground and the toadstools
drop their padded riot-gear.
A flower flows, a river flowers.
The moon's lard melts in its skillet.
There are a number of doors, each one at
the end of a road and each road has
a different quality. One leads through
the slug of despond, inbuilt bigender.
Molluch is the furthermoist affix
a neoplasm of purplexity
deboned bodybuilder elbow
greasing in sappiness, snogging
the flowers, horning leaves, rasping.
It trancetraces the christain squishrich
timedrags its clubfoot tonguestem
endgenders in dreambic eyefall
zeppeling the glazy inoceans.
There were women at windows
at twilight, appearing to look in mirrors
not visible to me, through whom I elongated.
They touched me on an intimate part of
my name, full of substance and gleam
as a lost appendage, a sixth toe.
The seacreatury of the treesury
riskassesses a fat tax for the lumpemployed
uneases his viscera, undistends.
I come out in the rain to find my
eyestalk backlogclogged my loam
foot selfseals a plowpath that
treacles the soul of a stone; am
expert in the nature of rain.

Bookworm

The novel begins: two travellers, seagull
and star, see the night bus run empty.
In dictionaries is defined what it is
we no longer have. A devil in the toenail
maths the voluminous timespace that
ends on the black of the page. Collapsed
Tetragrammaton bled out of word
and he explains in glosses that ladders
did not reach, in the attic books swarm
angrily from their boxes. Populations
surge: in their hooked hands is sand, siftwork,
the varioral textscape, unterwelten.
He shouts in his sleep he is stuck inside
time's tomefoolery awaiting the age of mildew.
His head has many spokesmen, heaven is
a timewarped scroll. The people incredulous:
they drilled the rubble to find a library
in cinderends, within it buried the word
for you, the past ill in your vast bed.
We had forgotten how the forest stretched
into a single twig or spire of dust.
Ghosts fit between pages, waiting for
the news to invent time to forget
eternity. The sparsim tararas
under the hardbacked carapace have eyes to hurt
myself with, a sense losing in the spill,
so sleep the words into the book, tunnel
a novel, erupt as bullethole among
the embers, unearthed reader, eat alive
the pronouns, think open the sensefolds:
all pages will be binding upon us.

Bedbug

I was a penis in my previous wife
plumping a tormulted skinurge
I cockscrewed my sensors in a thoughsand
sweat nosethings with raspeyes and secret
juices, minoture to an atomation
my fecifork felched roseflesh in bat
of the eyeless nudescending a stircease
she slept open my head and afar
voices when the door ajarred
surmounted the furnurture
scrawled over the coverletter
I fleshened my hemispears into
mouthhook to oilwell in limbage
as my entined inslider or genital mouth
in everesting faunication mine-
shafted into bitternest on the nerve
like exworkers in the exindustry
benightly a pistonish chinch
to prick a crimped plastron
with illwilling resistungs to emblody
the grozet throne with blaeber and some
thing in my dreams messed with me
illicit suckler of gubernation that
lovesickened the nightsweats
secrept the wounderer these are the
legintimate pictures blood makes as it
drowns its godheaded hook
and bedusted the entryways
massive-cocked rockstar I am not:
he who hinderstands the bedveil
wanks in the moltel of the eyeclot.

Snail

The snayle in his cotearmure cam in among
all other redy to fighte agayne this serpente.

The water breaks his face. He pushes it
out from sleep, in the rain, up the wall.
Prolapse of stout party. Shhe would be
our sex if we were both
felame and enamale,
a selfsamed seacreation
of the collapsible brainpit. S
he camareadies herhis nolensed cornicles.
What processed herm here is that h
she wants hisher eyes. Hisherits
silverse tongue longates a thinghinge
housing ornate flowerflows. Totteringly
they headvance their caravantankerous
motorhomes across maps of sleep with sputummy
crayons and selfpropel our conchtracts.
The hostile take-over birds enters
the garden discarding husks
there's a faintest possible moon and
fleeingly they shoehorn brainshell
lapse under two layers of emulsion
they tuck in bucket or flowerpot
rims, or sleep asunder past the thrush-
thrusted shelterrors. On our windows these
spendlid dulcesses of the earthear
squeegee the groundown malegazine
and mindstride its somehinge to return
like nevercut thumbnails, discarded
body-parts, ramparts, trails of self
and I fell to the grass under my feet,
thus animated the stone. Thought is hard.

Millipede

Do not be unarmed. We newsfeed out of
holes in stone to cog the clockword with threads
breadths under the moon's empire. The heart's earth
is cold, night tightens. Each car duplicates
silence. Text feelers its quernturned frills. In
my previous life I ran shadows, coiled to
the touch. My name was seep or bleed, not leaf.
Spines of ghosts towered inside me, money
slept in the cracks. Underclover agents
clung as I entered the meeting the pulse
dwindled in my legs, processionary
data I bore was null assuming streams
lipped that oak metropole my song throughed
whatever words came to burn away,
their shadows spoke into the dust. Rot and
growth fight inside a tree for centuries.
I understoned that refugee-capital
figured in cracked-open barks. The metachine
rootstemmed rollbacks fungible to
the eye and its depths as rains open the
smoke-cloaked oak's fallouts, each uniquery
no more than that seethe through cling of form
past firmamelts such as water sieve by
rust, agrainst the gain dreamsaw this hawksclaw
dustilling a rustangled illiterature
so deriddle me this: I live belowgro
underground with my sister: is she
exister, insister, or resister.
Where the water was as dead she stored
the captured rainbows and her feet make a line not
scan. Frilled like a chinese dragon she
tippled toiletwater and worried night's
skin, queried the leaf, thought the man who put
the stones in fruit did so to tell us something.
My claws cannot stop outside you, my pilled
head pieces togethers from your insides.

Giant Millipede

All roads are wider than long.
On the narrow path that became no track
in the Copper Canyon, lost,
painstaking a way down, on a ledge,
the evening in the leaves already, seeking
a place to camp, I came close to you
pocolocomotionally rounding
riverlong to ledgeland, hued of oilslick,
where the water was as dead and
rainbows were spaces I could not part,
remerembering the millelongated
etceteration that was illmelt by
meanlight zootalons of savagevisaged
train that clustered at my feet
swaying invoiceless to selfaddress
the serpoint of the turning worm
defining itself against night
turnturked its legprints into
animations of face that touched where
the air felt my thoughts abandoned.
Since I am unturning no stone there is
prescience in the sun declining to answer
it has no self even though a theory of mind is
gleam, the rust in the carapace
speaks of rubble that was a tower, the animals
smell dead in protocoils of language
when time wound the gates and throbbed
the subsoiled tonguestones, these are just
the films of people: they look like hell.

Sandhopper

Pigmyhop to the uninundated forestshore.
Seathedge the farthom that
holds the line against weed.
An infirmament of motile forkfolk
is heavening its leaflitteral tidalities
in weaved seasonglong: beach
flee, fission farthunder,
feast on edge of defalted bladders
& shredded casettetape
orasif to skipjack the unshore
in seaspraysprung piles. Dodgy pop
ups shore the undisonant
oozeless. There opined my
mouths and cry over spilt mind, in
the driftline of kneehigh scab,
timeuntidy eledgelies of feelbitten
foretime. All my jokes came true
the clouds out of breath
loose a trace against time.
O shards inside the dream awaken
complicate the language on
the brittle shore where text exceeds
meaning and sea is spokes
woman for the dead, cross
grain the seassaulted unboundaries
when I get to the borderline
fleckflock an antirational flapflup
saltate the surfface, the wrack
undersand we ununderstand
wereyou whitherwave the witherwells.

Crab

You cannot go into the room that you are in
when the sun paints purple at eventide gales
spend against Darwin's sinking forehead
coal-scuttlers clamp the tristopic water
gates the notes woven into the sea unsing
and layered among the mangraves selfsating
time, that metalegged revolverlover, cancers
the dancer and churns echoes to shoreshoes,
beats telesales into command-centres, backforms
trivet into tank-turret. O telescope-
eyed proctor, face inside the mask the sea
bed is barnacling into shape and you
cannot mind the voice that shelves cloud.
Pinch me if the seathru honourglass is sour-
souled, the porcelain chevalier with golden-
cuirassed arms mittens the oozean with
scrapy remotions, carapacing submargins
while Diogenes handfuls the wheels under.
Hold pursepose and irresoluble highflows
windlass pureprose that purls where you
put ground is world that contains not-me, mountain
of faulty mirrors and behinged mouth
palp dipping crossedly as a fiddler bows
in concert. Render to seizure the canned goods
go to open the water and the kelp
floats its interleaved occupants, floor
disharmed with tincantations and Troy-destroying
odes. With these you senseassess the skyfold
and sidestep the bones, as lightbeats to
and frolick you must remote-control
the eyestalk as godinself comes ashshore
in asymetrical deployment from a text on
sign, the slave of darkness, plexus
of voidance belettling the squenched dreamhole
as plianter counterfeet call you to arms

where stuff's upturnage cankers
the mandarin-faced wrong-heirs. Sate
upon this grotesquery othertheless
the professors of popetry unleave
your clockworks as you scarab down to sand
lockdowned into an unchanic slavery
that discants against your sealedin skin.
Your axes cannot break the frozen sea.

Worm

Raise the midden, cast the king
find where the stars hide from us.
Aganglionic in bed of state
asthrougnought the depthly
dissembloodies bodimelt.
We are no part of speech
but mud's fifth essence, slur
of strangurge that threadth
a tractile strengthin, inchforthing
annulets for which coagulate
dumbone is fleshlier beforeskin.
Maintaingling the whormament
evereverse the filesh and misinter
netherending phantomblims
as an intestinal spacebody.
Slack as a nonsible prosumer that
nightoils secreative tonguextensions
graveward we groundmother
to subterrest, intingling our
undertread in prolongable
rollongations. This is urned in
trunnels: wordroots gather in a rind
under hills where horses of great density
once ran and mostly the days
sleep in their boxes but the hurt
clouds still bruise. We are what
hills store in their batteries,
sutured guts that fuel birdsong.
To handle the dead harden your hands,
accost windows, expend stalked
figures. Night runs us down.

Threadworm

If an alien were to measure us and
take as most significant the microfauna,
disregarding sentience, seek then
the cave of sleep among the flowers of
Beulah. If language could reverse the state
thread your blood here. Things cling.
A word in its torn form is enough to
make the meat descend in lumps against
tarnish pools the mineral mind is literal in
the sense we forget how to heave. The sphincter's
riddle is that who hurts ignorance
is strange: roll the shadow out of the head,
it is too shaped. These are the dwellers
for whom we are dwelling; we entwine
with protoslimes. Outside the window
the smoke wounds ideographs, choirs
of watertight drinkers surround us
like coalchemists placing sibyllines
into the mouth of a golem. Frothever
the earthfarm, the winding up or end
of any soft springy substance, loose
heavy. Meet meat the corner a
feeling amounts and a sense nullfeels
its semantics in the place of excrement
play Boswell with backlogged anuscript
in measureless caverns big biotech likes you
stranded widthin the selflong endangland that
intestines the systemstem & bloodcurds in
order to induct the cavernacle's bleakage
it hookes open to egglay on gutted horifice.
Always suspect the history that centres
us is wrong, a spacecraft under our
eyes pulsates its tongueless urmurmur:
fatherhood, mothership, welling-place.

Sea slug

I did not feel that poets were using
language to the full extent of its in
scapability. Though she has no feet,
she clouds through spirit; ingestion tends
to the self-substantial, its other wound
drowns. She has no back and bends her head
backwards/ she has no thin skin and instals
deceits, membrum at night, feeding on
subtile derangements her laminate
flesh is hair to, animate on the milk-
stained stone filterfeeds as underangel
whereby her gillslits glisten in labial
unction, process swart light in realmy
sea beds sunctioned by undulation
whereforest involutions of intestine
synthesize the sun with stolen indigenes
moves pithed root but having fallen
is sluggish, obeys aether's nature,
eggcysts in the limblimp invagination
mopmops the notochord's senseaccordion
writes the answer in distracts of gas
plasma. Wetward lividity booms in
relishquish of unstone, piles through kelps.
Abstracts the crab from its raggy bed.
No prizes, love is the universal
act, gilttipped headsets pass over
peopled stone, shadow's tide
lilyfrilled in sensate state hardens
flowever's lipsmudged sunblights
sifting the mulchlike snows, down
to the starlight's silts' nightly rain.

Leech

All things that love the sun are out of doors.
Eyes have not been thought of, we are as meat
to sail day light, dense limbs of rain can wind
at the end of the tongue. It is hard for
the star of earth to binge drink in warp space
like one whom I had met with in a dream.
Form who can sun flesh peach the while round us
thins. In dim things clouds of is seep flame, per
son whose mask speaks through scream is at the end
had in mind those wheels of flesh through whom I
could see the earth brim. It sucks the blood of
man & beast & bides the place that it sucks
till it be full & then falls, the world in
the grain of slime, the lane of the dad that
lights to the touch is left to state but how
the well are in flames. We changed in mid flow
to stream of hedge when light is seal of self
that will spring from its page and sink its long
and sharp tooth in to your eyes and suck and
then sink in a soup that is half shade as
the light fixed things, we are the long dead, our
eyes are built from seeds of this a drunk arm
from pond to pond he roams from moor to moor
far from the world I walk, and from all care.
The grass is bright with rain drops on the moors.
I bared my froth forth to blanch at the sight
build for him, sow for him, and at his care
scroop or rasp the quicked purr of dead pome, sieved
is seethe, what seeps tolls the zoo starts here slurp
on the spilt sperm ghost rain dance like a grub
a flute of foulth frig your glans with smur and
wrought things as light of puff to see through this
world next world to the last, chuck a ream of scrab
but now his voice to me is like a stream
the gleamt gawp husks left in the lurch is flip
like a sea beast crawled forth, that on a shelf
creak in to a new flop hum a song of.

Tapeworm

Fruitless for the academic tapeworm to horde its excrementa in books.

Each object deserves its own word.
Neologize this snowflak, the crustal crystal,
particicle, idling immachinery, emptiny
eyerime where the ropes lessen and
intertwine, the cloak of mangy colours
singularity of light, crop, ear, hornclogged
fluke of nurture, enclayed deathcycle, schizoid
saltlick, crown of hooks, hook or crook of zoa
contiguous and palapable infirmament
in deceived unhand of mentation
urinetinged the metallurge corevice
of the abundulant alterworld
that fleshholds the deathread to
selflengthen by suffixation, head by head
the lips heal closed the fragments are thin
king between them as pieces freeze
above seas that eviscerate the skullhull,
prelongating an unself intimater
of dreamholes as the sky flexes its
moon, asks who am I a list of?
or if it rained punctuation what
is made love of the bodies dreaming us
relaxed then dried with their heads bent.
We have nothing to buy-back but our chains.
If the afterworld of the artwork be liquid
poems need headroom and armrest, legend
and kneedeep: but are you not active in
the spirit-world, the lid of nature
in the head lists, poem self-perpetuates
the wound, desire armed to the sixth side of god
caves in a colorectal christmother
methought it embowels the head-being
of an enchained pharaon swallowed in that night
who is codepiece of the awkwork circlet

the toilless antiking is merchanical sublimator
host-seeking eggsegments that encyst
upon the gutstring kindly death unsets us.
I open my head to you, starter of wars and
water of stars, your outshat head winks back.

Paper Shale

It is snowing stone: flocks of flecks
halfcircle and downfall sea-
through waves roughly troughing;
glass-hearted seafleas snorkel
bladderwracky cryptoscapes and cog
down as diatomic snow, as nows'
succumbing accumulations, flailing
wrongfootedly to subluminal depth
flitwise and in hindlight
each an icarus descending with
cold-compressed seapage of punctilious
and angelhaired headpieces, downwards
scribbledehobble of billowly
dodecadragons, aqualunged
legs, chitinny leg-ends,
slivery and lipletted apparencies.
In a siftless night of flitting cogitators
whitespread the pollenchanted scalewings
are fantangled in photic jettrails.
Descend further, to darks parted
by flashlit circumfauna. It is
written they are all gone in
to the dark, squidink blots and
sesameseed-sized sputnicks
that pearlmutate the petalface eyepiece.
Then the print the hum of stone settling,
motes, motets, as ash or as
the next word to rain onto the floor
beneath the one we stand on, impressing
into bedrock the chalkblack
precipitants, eventless paleoslope
denizened by ghosts captured in
a massbook, written under seapressure
by the old and the dying, all that falls
cleaving the leaftime of its scripture.

www.ingramcontent.com/pod-product-compliance
Lightning Source LLC
Chambersburg PA
CBHW031154160426
43193CB00008B/358